good food
FOR ALL
seasonal recipes from a community garden

About The Stop

Located in Toronto's west end, The Stop works to increase access to food in a manner that maintains dignity, builds health and community and challenges inequality. From its origins as one of Canada's first food banks, The Stop has blossomed into a thriving community hub where neighbours participate in a broad range of programs that provide healthy food, as well as foster social connections, build food skills and promote engagement in civic issues. Among the busy initiatives are community kitchens and gardens, cooking classes, drop-in meals, peri-natal support, a food bank, outdoor bake ovens, food markets and community advocacy. In 2009, The Stop opened The Green Barn, a sustainable food production and education centre with a 3,000-square-foot greenhouse, commercial kitchen, classroom, sheltered garden and composting facility. School visits and an after-school program offer hands-on opportunities for children to learn about the food system. Underlying all of The Stop's efforts is the view that food should be a basic human right.

www.thestop.org

First trade paperback edition September 2009

Designed by Ruth Alves
Photography by Jodi Pudge, James Tse, Laura Berman & Anna Prior
Food Stylist Lindsay Evans
Prop Stylist & Food Stylist Madeleine Johari

Manufactured in the United States of America

10 9 8 7 6 5 4 3 2 1

ISBN 978-1-4391-7041-0

To the community members of The Stop,
who, as leaders in the struggle to create
a more just and healthy food system,
inspired this cookbook.

table of contents

Foreword

There's a revolution happening in the world of food. Chefs, environmentalists, journalists, activists, parents and foodies of all stripes have begun to make a powerful case for the benefits of fresh food sourced from sustainable local farms and artisans. The reasons are legion: it's more nutritious, doesn't require as much fossil fuel to get to our tables and just plain tastes better. Buying local also supports the efforts of regional farmers and preserves growing space.

But this revolution has too often seemed a middle-class concern, with local and sustainably produced food just another privilege of the wealthy. For 30 years, The Stop, an innovative non-profit organization in the heart of one of Toronto's poorest and most under-serviced neighbourhoods, has been working to ensure that low-income people also have a voice and a stake in this social movement. We believe that a just food system has a place for everyone at the table.

With programs ranging from gardens to a drop-in café, from a health initiative for low-income pregnant women to a food bank, from peer advocacy to cooking classes for adults and children alike, The Stop uses food as a powerful tool to build hope, health, skills and community.

We see just how powerful it can be every day: in our gardens and greenhouse, where people from vastly different cultural backgrounds — recent immigrants and those who've been in Canada for generations, young families and homeless men — grow food together and learn about one another's lives and challenges. We see it in our community kitchens, where people share their knowledge and learn how healthy eating can be their best defence against debilitating diet-related illnesses like diabetes and cardiovascular disease. We also see it when our volunteers translate their experience at The Stop into paid work.

Having started in the mid-1970s as a food bank in a downtown church, we have grown into an internationally respected organization with a powerful mission: to promote healthy food and universal access to it.

So it's no accident that the title of this beautiful new cookbook — based on recipes developed at our centre by The Stop's Joshna Maharaj — is *Good Food for All*. Both a statement and a battle cry, it perfectly expresses what The Stop is all about.

Good Food for All not only celebrates fresh, seasonal food and healthy eating, it also aims to raise awareness about the connections between food and social justice, health, the environment and community. We hope that in these pages you'll find both inspiration for some great meals and encouragement to question the dominant food system, a system whose fault lines are showing more and more: in the worldwide obesity epidemic; in food safety problems that pop up in the news on a daily basis; in the environmental degradation caused by vast factory farms. We hope that after reading about the potential of good food to bring people together and to promote the health of both communities and individuals, you will join us in calling for greater food justice in your own neighbourhood and across the globe.

At The Stop, we think the good food revolution is a tremendous opportunity. Because food connects us all. *–Nick Saul, Executive Director, The Stop*

A Note from the Kitchen

My first day in the kitchen at The Stop was overwhelming, to say the least. Our program director laid out what seemed like some sort of reality TV challenge: make a healthy lunch for 150 people on a minimal budget using a small team of volunteers with varying levels of kitchen skills — in three hours. I took a deep breath and got to work.

It has been more than three years since that first day. There have been many successes and a few disasters along the way, but within those challenging parameters we have found a way to make it work. I can proudly say our kitchen has become a little utopia, producing delicious, wholesome food that is easy to make, with ingredients that are both affordable and readily available.

Fortunately, The Stop community has embraced my cooking and my style of food. Some were harder to win over than others, but most people appreciate good, healthy food. Thinking about the difference between our kitchen and those of our participants, I realized the answer was simple: knowledge. When you know how to cook, you can turn even the humblest ingredients into a good meal. You can't have food security if you don't have food skills. You don't need a lot of money to eat well, but you do need some knowledge and confidence in the kitchen, and that's where this cookbook comes in.

I'm convinced the best way to become a good cook is to develop your intuition about food, which means getting into the kitchen, putting an apron on and getting busy. Learn about ingredients, how they interact with each other and how they react to heat, air and water. And be prepared for the occasional disaster — cooking is all about trial and error.

If you can, plant a garden, too. With so much bounty, you'll have no choice but to cook! Then you'll want to share it with others, and so many good things will follow.

Good Food for All is all about collaboration. The recipes in this book are rooted in our programming at The Stop, with contributions from our staff, volunteers, participants and community at large; they represent the diversity of our neighbourhood and of our city.

The recipes also embrace local, seasonal eating, and you should be able to find these affordable, wholesome ingredients at farmers' markets and in most large grocery stores. We've tried to make the directions simple and easy to follow, but please feel free to experiment. To that end, we have included lots of tips and notes on seasonality and substitutions — after all, improvisation is at the heart of our approach to food at The Stop.

We hope this book will offer you a new way to think about food and the ways it can enrich our lives. From The Stop's kitchen to yours, we extend the hope that you will embrace the pleasure of cooking good food and sharing it with others — and that someday soon everyone will have a seat at the table.

–Joshna Maharaj, Chef

Pantry

Stocking your Kitchen

Here are some helpful hints from our kitchen to get you well stocked and ready to cook delicious, healthful food. Of course, this is just the beginning: we encourage you to find a system that works for you and the kind of cooking you do.

Fats
We use a small range of fats generously but not excessively, and avoid heavily processed ones.

Butter tastes great, but is fairly expensive and burns easily. That said, butter adds rich flavour to foods and lends a texture to baked goods that other fats simply cannot replicate. We use unsalted butter in our kitchen so we can control the amount of salt in the final product. Go ahead and use salted butter if it's all you have, but reduce the salt in the recipe to compensate. We encourage you to stay as far away from margarine as you can. It is so highly processed that many of us feel it does more damage than a bit of saturated fat.

Vegetable oil is a great multi-purpose fat that doesn't cost a lot and tastes pretty good. We use sunflower and canola oil for stir-fries, shallow and deep-frying, and on the griddle. **Extra-virgin olive oil** is a slightly more expensive oil that is packed with nutrition and adds great flavour to almost anything you sauté; it is also the base for most of our vinaigrettes. Occasionally we use **grapeseed oil**, which has a really clean taste, a high smoking point and many of the same health benefits as olive oil. It is, however, more expensive. Use the best quality you can afford.

Acids
Whether you favour vinegar or lemon juice, acids are an essential component of a well-stocked pantry. They help tenderize foods, provide brightness, and balance the other flavours in your dish. We use **cider**, **balsamic** and **rice vinegars** and fresh **lemon juice** most frequently in our kitchen. Cider vinegar is versatile and quite healthful; balsamic is sweeter and full-bodied; rice vinegar is gentle and light. And nothing beats the tang of a lemon.

Salt and Pepper
We use **kosher salt**; except in baking and desserts. Its grains are larger and you can actually see how much you're using. Keep a little bowlful beside your stovetop and use your fingers to dispense it so you really get a feel for seasoning. Kosher salt also has a lower density of sodium, which means you have more control over the amount of sodium you add.

We grind our own **peppercorns** because there is nothing like the bright flavour of freshly cracked pepper. We use a coffee grinder dedicated to spices; wooden twist grinders work beautifully too.

Herbs and Spices

Whenever possible, we use **fresh herbs**. That said, dried bay leaves, thyme, oregano, rosemary and basil are used often in our kitchen, particularly in spice rubs, cold-weather soups, stews and casseroles. We also use a wide variety of whole spices in our kitchen. You'll get more flavour out of them if you toast and grind whole seeds into powder (that dedicated spice grinder again). Heat a dry skillet on medium-high heat. Add whole spices and toast, turning constantly, until fragrant (they can burn quickly, so pay close attention). Transfer to your spice grinder and grind to a powder. Dried herbs and spices generally have about a six-month shelf life. Store in airtight containers in a dry and relatively cool place.

Sweeteners

Sweetness is an essential component to good cooking, and we encourage you to try different sources in their purest form. **Brown sugar**, **honey** and **maple syrup** are the most commonly used sweeteners in our kitchen. You can almost always replace refined white sugar with brown sugar, but it will alter the colour and texture of the final product, adding a molasses flavour and more weight. There is complexity and diversity in sweet flavours, and we love finding ways to incorporate local maple syrup and honey in our cooking.

Grains

Whenever possible, use whole grains. We have found **brown rice** and **whole wheat pasta** to be quite affordable and widely available, as well as **bulgur** and **whole wheat couscous. Spelt flour** is a favourite of ours, as it can replace all-purpose flour in the same quantity in muffins, cookies and quick breads. At some farmers' markets, you can find some really beautiful local grains. Buying local organic **whole wheat flour** can have a dramatic impact on the flavour and structure of your baking.

Produce

Best-case scenario, we'd all be able to get our hands on local organic fruit and vegetables, but our limited growing season and the higher cost of organics make things a bit challenging. Perhaps the most important bit of information we can share with you is this: **local trumps organic**. It's a much better idea to buy local conventional produce than organic produce that's been flown in. Nurturing our local food economies is the only way they'll grow, so do yourself a favour: find a farmers' market in your area and visit regularly. Our farmers need all the love they can get, and they have an incredible wealth of knowledge and experience to share.

There is also a profound satisfaction that comes from **growing your own food**. A home garden provides the shortest distance from field to table and supplements your household food budget. Plus, letting your garden dictate what you eat will inspire creativity in your kitchen. We all need to get more involved in the growing of our food and the stewardship of our land.

Meat and Fish

From the inferior-quality feed that many conventionally raised animals are given to the environmental impact of raising and slaughtering livestock and processing meat, there are many good reasons to rethink our meat consumption. There are two steps in this process: **eating less meat** and **shopping carefully for the meat we do eat**. There is no question about the virtue of local, naturally raised meat. So shop with your eyes open — read labels or ask where meat comes from. Still, naturally raised meat is expensive, which forces many of us to go the conventional route. But you can make it more affordable by seeking out less expensive cuts — they're often a bit tougher or still have skin and/or bones attached, but they're so flavourful and quite easy to prepare.

Here in Southern Ontario, fresh fish is a luxury. We don't serve fish or seafood often at The Stop, but when we do, we get the freshest stuff we can. Farmers' markets are a great source of locally raised fish, as are city fishmongers. Just remember: with fish, fresh is always best.

Equipment

Although we have a pretty well-equipped commercial kitchen at The Stop, the recipes in this book can certainly be made without any fancy gadgets or appliances. The way we see it, we had good food before there were stand mixers and zesters, so don't be deterred if you've got minimal kitchen equipment — you can do this! We will suggest one thing: get your hands on a reasonably **good chef's knife** and keep it sharp. Sharp knives make cooking easy and joyful. Also, **parchment paper** is one indulgence we allow ourselves. It keeps things from sticking to your pans and prevents you having to do any major scrubbing.

Here is a list of the basic equipment we use in this book:

- chef's knife
- non-stick sauté pan
- mixing bowls (in varying sizes)
- colander
- cutting board
- saucepan
- stockpot
- stainless steel sauté pan
- baking sheet
- 9- x 13-inch baking dish
- wire whisk
- wooden spoons
- rubber spatula
- tongs
- ladle
- measuring spoons
- liquid and dry measuring cups
- food processor or immersion blender
- kitchen towels/oven mitts

Now, let's talk about stoves and ovens. Our dream kitchen has a gas stove and a convection oven. Gas gives you strong, instant heat. Convection uses the heat in the oven more efficiently by circulating it around. This helps your baked goods rise higher, it helps things brown and crisp more evenly, and it often cuts down considerably on the cooking time. If you've got a conventional oven and an electric coil stovetop, don't despair. You'll do just fine. Just pay closer attention to things in the oven, rotating them to even out the browning if necessary.

asparagus beets
carrots cucumber
radishes parsnips
fiddleheads leeks
sweet peppers peas
lettuce mushrooms
green onions **spring**
parsnips cabbage
rhubarb potatoes
strawberries

Spring Awakening

In early spring, our community gardens are carpeted in snow. We spend hours poring over seed catalogues, dreaming of brightly coloured heirloom tomatoes and peppers, drawing and redrawing the garden plans in order to find a place for them all. The seeds, like the people who plant them, come from all over. Some will take root spontaneously, like the tomatillos and the Jerusalem artichokes. Others, like one rare variety of Sicilian eggplant, exchange hands over a neighbour's fence. It really does take a community to grow a garden.

Planting a garden in springtime is one of the best things you can do for your kitchen. It doesn't have to be big: even a few pots on the windowsill, filled with mint and chives, are an economical way to add spring flavour to salads and pastas. Start a few tomato seedlings, and your modest investment will pay dividends come summertime. Think you don't have the space? Chef Lorenzo Loseto has grown just about everything he needs for his busy downtown Toronto kitchen in old recycling bins on a sliver of a balcony above George Restaurant: peppers, tomatoes, lettuce, zucchini, even watermelons. Many came from seedlings that were cultivated in our gardens.

It really does take a community to grow a garden.

Our growing season begins at The Stop's Green Barn, an old streetcar maintenance facility that's been reinvented as a sustainable food production and education centre with a 3,000-square-foot temperate greenhouse. In March, the signs of promise are everywhere: pots and flats stacked in tall columns, rolls of masking tape and markers ready for labelling. Finally, the schoolchildren stream into the greenhouse, excited to fill pots with dark soil and seeds.

For a cook intent on following the seasons, spring can be the greatest challenge. As the days begin to lengthen and the sun grows stronger, we crave the lean, clean flavours of asparagus and rhubarb. But the wait seems eternal in March and April, when maple syrup is the only local food in season.

Before we know it, though, Rhonda and her crew of gardeners are bringing wheelbarrows of chives to the kitchen. Chive pesto (page 43) is a great way to preserve the excess; it even freezes well. Generous neighbours are knocking on the door, offering us the precious bunches of wild leeks they've foraged in city parks. (Some of the best things in life really are free.)

Each week brings something new and something green, from spinach that tastes truly earthy and full-flavoured to those fat, sweet spears of peak-season asparagus. Soup made from French sorrel, a green leaf with a sour taste, has the schoolkids in hysterics. "It tastes like I'm drinking green apple!" says one. Then finally, just as spring turns to summer, a local farmer drops by on his way back from the market, generously offering his unsold baskets of strawberries. Like all foods, the sun-ripened berries taste better when they're shared. –*Sasha Chapman*

Seafood Chowder

One day we received a rare donation of some frozen fish and seafood, and this was the best way we could think of to extend it and serve a large number of people. You could see everyone's eyes widen with surprise when they read the day's menu. We served it with cheddar herb muffins (page 22).

Ingredients

8 bacon slices, chopped

2 large onions, chopped

4 8-oz (250 mL) bottles clam juice

4 cups ½ -inch-dice peeled white potatoes (about 3 lb/1.5 kg)

4 cups ½ -inch-dice peeled butternut squash (about 3 lb/1.5 kg)

2 bay leaves

5 cups milk

1 cup half-and-half cream

2 tbsp minced fresh thyme or 2 tsp dried, crumbled

hot sauce, like Frank's or Tabasco, to taste

1 lb (500 g) mixed fresh fish (a choice of cod, halibut, haddock and/or scrod), cut into ¾ -inch pieces

1 lb (500 g) large* raw shrimp, thawed, peeled and deveined

1 lb (500 g) sea scallops, patted dry

Large shrimp (16 to 20 count per pound)

Method

1. To render fat, cook bacon in a large, heavy saucepan over medium-high heat for 5 minutes. Add onions and sauté until they are translucent, about 8 minutes. Mix in clam juice, potatoes, squash and bay leaves. Simmer 5 minutes. Add milk, cream and thyme. Simmer until vegetables are almost tender, about 10 minutes.

2. Add fish, shrimp and scallops and simmer until cooked through, about 3 minutes. Season to taste with salt and pepper and a dash (or more!) of hot sauce. Discard bay leaves.

Serves 8

Cheddar Herb Muffins

Here are the muffins that were so good with our seafood chowder on page 20. With this recipe it's easy to produce simple, freshly baked goodies for a crowd. If you have only one muffin pan, just keep the remaining batter aside until the first batch is done. Re-oil the pan if necessary.

Ingredients

½ cup vegetable oil,
plus more for pan

2 cups all-purpose flour

2 cups whole wheat flour

2 tbsp granulated sugar

2½ tsp baking powder

1 tsp baking soda

1 tsp dried sage

1 cup chopped fresh parsley

1 cup grated cheddar cheese

2½ cups buttermilk

2 large eggs

Method

1. Preheat oven to 400°F. Brush 2 muffin tins lightly with oil and set aside. In a large bowl, combine flours, sugar, baking powder, baking soda, sage, parsley and cheese; blend well.

2. In a separate bowl, blend buttermilk, oil and eggs. Add to dry mixture and stir just until moistened. Fill greased muffin tins two-thirds full.

3. Bake for 15 to 20 minutes, or until a wooden toothpick inserted into the centre of a muffin comes out clean. Remove from oven. Let cool completely on wire rack.

Makes 24

Broccoli Leek Soup

The bright onion flavour of leeks pairs really well with sweet broccoli, and leeks and butter are old friends. But to avoid the cost and saturated fat of all that butter, we've used it in combination with oil. Feel free to substitute vegetable stock for the chicken stock, or even water in a pinch.

Ingredients

2 tbsp vegetable oil

1 tbsp butter

2 bunches fresh broccoli, stems and florets separated and chopped into bite-size pieces

2 leeks, white and light green parts only, washed and finely sliced

2 garlic cloves, minced

1 russet potato, peeled and diced

6½ cups chicken stock or canned low-salt chicken broth

kosher salt and freshly ground pepper

1 cup grated extra-sharp cheddar cheese

Method

1. Heat oil and butter in a heavy, medium pot over medium-high heat. Add broccoli stems and leeks and season lightly with salt; sauté until onion is translucent, about 6 minutes. Add garlic and sauté 1 minute. Add florets, potato and stock; bring to a boil. Reduce heat and simmer, uncovered, until vegetables are tender, about 15 minutes.

2. Remove from heat and, using an immersion blender, blend soup until completely smooth and lump free. Return to heat and simmer to reduce soup, if necessary. Taste and adjust seasoning as necessary. Serve with a nice pile of grated cheese on top and enjoy!

Serves 6

Quinoa with Asparagus, Peas and Feta

Quinoa is an ancient grain that is nearly a complete protein as well. It has a delicious nuttiness and is probably one of the most wholesome things you can eat. Treat it just like any other grain, and experiment with flavour.

Ingredients

⅓ cup extra-virgin olive oil

2 tbsp red wine vinegar

1 tbsp Dijon mustard

1 clove garlic, minced

kosher salt and freshly ground pepper

3 cups quinoa

½ bunch asparagus, ends trimmed, chopped into 1-inch pieces

1 cup frozen green peas

1 cup cubed feta cheese (optional)

Method

1. Whisk together olive oil, vinegar, mustard and garlic in a small bowl. Season with salt and pepper and set aside.

2. Bring a medium-sized pot of salted water to a boil. Meanwhile, wash quinoa well under running water. Add quinoa to boiling water and cook about 10 minutes, or until the little tails pop out and each grain is tender but still intact. Strain in a colander and rinse really well with cool water to stop the cooking. Set aside to drain.

3. Bring a small saucepan of water to a boil. Fill a medium bowl with ice water and have it close to the stove. When the water is at a rolling boil, add a generous pinch of salt and the asparagus. Cook for 1 minute, until the green of the asparagus brightens and pieces become tender. Remove from pot and plunge into ice water immediately to stop the cooking. Repeat this process with frozen peas. Strain vegetables and set aside.

4. Place quinoa in a large bowl and drizzle with 2/3 of vinaigrette; season with salt and pepper and toss gently. Add asparagus, peas, feta and remaining vinaigrette and toss to combine. Taste and adjust seasoning as necessary.

Serves 6

The Mighty Grain Salad

This is an incredibly versatile recipe, one that provides the framework to build some delicious salads out of whatever you have on hand or feel like eating. The key is to keep tasting, and then adding elements to balance the flavour. Take the time to chop your vegetables into a small dice... you'll be rewarded with a very beautiful and complex mouthful.

Ingredients

2 cups cooked grain (bulgar, couscous, quinoa, barley, wheat berries, etc.), see grain cooking guide, page 28

2–3 tbsp oil (olive, canola, grapeseed, sunflower)

1–2 tbsp acid (vinegar, citrus juice)

2 tsp total of any desired spices such as cumin, coriander, paprika, turmeric or curry powder

kosher salt and freshly ground pepper

2 cups finely diced vegetables (peppers, cucumber, celery, carrot, etc.)

1 small handful each scallions and herbs (parsley, chives, fresh cilantro, dill, etc.), finely chopped

1 19-oz (540 mL) can beans (kidney beans, chickpeas, white beans, black beans, etc.), rinsed

1 handful toasted nuts or seeds (pumpkin seeds, pecans, almonds, etc.)

1 handful dried fruit (cranberries, raisins, chopped apricots, etc.)

1 small handful crumbled feta or goat cheese

Method

1. Place cooled, cooked grains in a large bowl and add oil, acid and spices; season generously with salt and pepper and toss well to combine. (You will want to overseason this mixture so that when you add the other ingredients, everything will catch some of that flavour.)

2. Add vegetables, scallions, herbs, beans, nuts or seeds, dried fruit and cheese and toss well to combine. Taste and adjust seasoning as necessary to produce a balanced and delicious flavour.

Serves 4 as a side

Tip

Toasting nuts and seeds: Preheat oven to 350°F. Spread nuts or seeds on a baking sheet and toast until lightly browned and fragrant (this can range from 7 to 19 minutes). Keep your eye on them, because they'll burn easily.

Grain Cooking Guide

Filling	Liquid to Grain Ratio	Method
bulgur	2:1	Add boiling broth/water and salt to bulgur in a bowl, cover with plastic wrap and let sit for 15 to 20 minutes, until all of the liquid has been absorbed. Fluff with a fork.
wheat berries	4:1	Rinse well. Bring salted water to a boil, then add grain and boil until grains are tender, about 10 minutes. Drain well in a colander.
quinoa	4:1	Rinse well and agitate quinoa under running water to remove bitterness, drain. Bring salted water to a boil, then add quinoa and boil until grains are tender and little tails have popped out, about 10 minutes. Drain well in a colander.
couscous*	1:1	Add boiling broth/water and salt to couscous in a bowl, cover with plastic wrap and let sit for 15 to 20 minutes, until all of the liquid has been absorbed. Fluff with a fork.
white rice**	2:1	Preheat oven to 350°F. Place rice in oven-proof casserole dish, add salt and water. Cover with foil and cook for about 30 minutes, until all of the liquid has been absorbed. Remove from heat and allow to sit 10 minutes. Fluff with a fork.**
brown rice**	3:1	Preheat oven to 350°F. Place rice in oven-proof casserole dish, add salt and water. Cover with foil and cook for about 45 minutes, until all of the liquid has been absorbed. Remove from heat and allow to sit 10 minutes. Fluff with a fork.**
jasmine/ basmati rice	2:1	Preheat oven to 350°F. Rinse rice well, until water runs mostly clear. Place rice in oven-proof casserole dish, add salt and water. Cover with foil and cook for about 30 minutes, until all of the liquid has been absorbed. Remove from heat and allow to sit 10 minutes. Fluff with a fork.**

* Couscous is not technically a grain, it's actually a pasta.
** Cooking rice in the oven is an easy, no-fail method, which works really well for large quantities. Feel free to use any stovetop method you are comfortable with instead, if you prefer.

Breakfast Burritos

We made these burritos to fuel community members before a march to the office of our member of provincial parliament, and then onward to Queen's Park for a day of action against poverty. You gotta feed the revolution! These would be a great lunch option too.

Ingredients

8 large eggs

2 scallions, finely chopped

1 red bell pepper, seeded and finely diced

⅓ cup milk

kosher salt and freshly ground pepper

2–3 tbsp butter

4 large whole wheat tortillas

store-bought salsa

1 ½ cups grated cheddar cheese

Method

1. In a mixing bowl, combine eggs, scallions, red pepper and milk. Season well with salt and pepper, and whisk to break up yolks. Heat butter over medium heat in a frying pan.

2. Add egg mixture and cook gently, moving it around the pan as it scrambles. Remove from heat and allow to cool slightly.

3. Lay tortillas out on the counter. Divide scrambled eggs evenly among tortillas, then top with salsa and cheese. Roll up tightly and serve.

Serves 4

Classy Tuna Sandwiches

Much like a salsa, tuna salad is best when you take the time to finely chop all the vegetables so that each bite is full and flavourful. The gherkins add the perfect salty-sweet crunch.

Ingredients

1 6-oz (170 g) can chunk tuna in water, drained

½ stalk celery, very finely diced

½ carrot, peeled and grated

2 gherkins or cornichons, very finely diced

1 scallion, finely chopped

1 tbsp very finely chopped fresh parsley or dill

juice of ½ lemon

2 tbsp mayonnaise

kosher salt and freshly ground pepper

4 slices whole wheat or multi-grain bread

1 handful salad greens

8 slices cucumber

Method

1. Combine tuna, celery, carrot, gherkins, scallion, parsley or dill, lemon juice and mayonnaise in a bowl. Season with salt and pepper and stir well to mix. Taste and adjust seasoning as necessary.

2. Divide tuna mixture between 2 slices of bread and pat down slightly. Arrange 4 cucumber slices on each layer of tuna and top with salad greens. Cover with second slice of bread and press down slightly. Slice sandwiches and serve.

Serves 2

Environment

When it comes to making sustainable food choices, it often seems as if there are more questions than answers. Local or organic? Certified or not? Free-range or free-run eggs? It's enough to make you throw up your hands. Never mind that you may be looking for the cheapest thing at the supermarket, in which case the environmental impact of grass-fed versus corn-fed beef may seem entirely beside the point.

It's incredibly complicated, but at The Stop we feel strongly that everyone deserves good, healthy food, and that affordability and sustainability can — and should — be compatible. Supporting good farming practices and stewardship of the earth that feeds us is everyone's responsibility. That's why we use our purchasing power to buy produce from local farmers. We also run a thriving farmers' market at The Green Barn and host a Good Food Market at our main site, making fresh produce available at wholesale prices for those on low incomes.

And no place is more affordable or sustainable than the garden. At The Stop, our three gardens (including a 3,000-square-foot temperate greenhouse) are a symbol of what's possible when a community puts on its gardening gloves. Each year, we harvest more than 5,000 pounds of organic produce to feed our many programs.

But even as we work to increase access to healthy, sustainably produced food in our own neighbourhood, we also think about the bigger environmental picture. We want government to support urban farms, improve local food infrastructure and preserve green belts of prime agricultural land around our cities. We urge politicians to rethink their support of the current food system, which depends heavily on fossil fuels. If anyone deserves government support, it's the farmers who grow our food sustainably, with minimal impact on the land.

There aren't many arenas of life where the most ethical choice is the most pleasurable one. But when it comes to eating, the best-tasting food is often produced most sustainably. Nobody can afford to be a purist all the time. But that's the great thing about food. You can tackle the issue one ingredient at a time. –*S.C.*

Spicy Peanut Noodles

You can use linguine or rice stick noodles for this recipe; soba noodles would be delicious, too. We have also substituted almond butter for peanut butter with great success. Sambal oelek is a red chili sauce that can be found in Asian grocery stores and markets, and brings a fresh, clean heat to this sauce. Serve this dish alone or paired with some quick-sautéed bok choy or other Asian greens.

Ingredients

1 ½ cups smooth peanut butter

½ cup rice vinegar

water

2 tsp sambal oelek, or to taste

5 – 6 cloves garlic, minced

1 large handful fresh cilantro, chopped

½ cup low-sodium soy sauce

2 tbsp honey or brown sugar

kosher salt

1 lb (500 g) noodles (linguine, rice stick, soba, etc.)

Method

1. Combine peanut butter, rice vinegar and about 1/2 cup water in a medium-sized bowl and whisk together to break down peanut butter, Add sambal, garlic, cilantro, soy sauce and honey; continue whisking, adding water bit by bit, until a loose, thick consistency is achieved. You want this to be pourable, otherwise it will not coat your noodles well. Taste, adding salt and adjusting seasoning as necessary. Set aside.

2. Cook noodles according to package directions. Drain well and run cold water through the noodles, tossing gently, to stop cooking process. Transfer to a large mixing bowl.

3. Add 2/3 of peanut sauce mixture to noodles and toss gently to combine. Try not to break up the noodles with your tossing. Add remaining sauce bit by bit until noodles are all coated.

Serves 4 to 6

Akiwenzies' Smoked Fish Pie

We received a generous donation of smoked Georgian Bay trout from the Akiwenzie family after The Green Barn Farmers' Market one day. The Akiwenzies have been fishing in Georgian Bay for generations. Andrew Akiwenzie recommended we make a fish pie and gave us some rough instructions, and with a bit of research, we came up with this recipe. The dish was nothing short of spectacular. For vegetarians, we substituted caramelized fennel for the fish to equally rave reviews.

Ingredients

2 lb (1 kg) Yukon Gold potatoes, washed

½ cup butter

salt and freshly ground black pepper

4 eggs

2 lb (1 kg) smoked fish, flaked into chunks

2 tbsp chopped flat-leaf parsley

¼ cup unsalted butter

¼ cup all-purpose flour

3 cups milk

pinch freshly grated nutmeg

1 cup grated Gruyère or cheddar cheese

Method

1. Place potatoes in a saucepan with a generous pinch of salt and cover with water. Bring potatoes to a boil, then simmer for 10 minutes, or until tender.

2. Drain potatoes and rinse to cool. Peel potatoes, using a tea towel to hold them if they're too hot to handle. Place potatoes in a bowl and mash until smooth, adding the 1/2 cup butter in bits as you mash. Season with salt and pepper and set aside.

3. Bring a small pan of water to a gentle boil. Carefully lower eggs into the water and boil for 8 minutes. Drain and cool eggs under cold water, then peel and cut into chunks.

4. In a 9- x 13-inch baking pan or casserole dish, spread fish and eggs in a single layer. Sprinkle with parsley. Preheat oven to 350°F.

5. In a saucepan, melt the unsalted butter, stir in flour and cook over a moderate heat for 1 minute. Gradually add milk, whisking constantly, and simmer for 1 to 2 minutes, until mixture starts to thicken and almost comes to a boil.

6. Remove sauce from heat, season with salt, pepper and nutmeg; pour over fish and eggs in dish.

7. Arrange mashed potato over the sauce, score with a fork to make a pretty pattern and sprinkle with grated cheese.

8. Bake for about 30 minutes, until bubbling and golden brown on top. Serve immediately.

Serves 6 to 8

Grilled Steak with Lemon Asparagus

This steak is a perfect spring dinner, and a squeeze of fresh lemon on nicely grilled asparagus is a little bit of heaven.

Ingredients

1½ lb (750 g) strip loin, sirloin or flank steak (see tip)

2 cloves garlic, minced

1–2 red chilies, minced

zest of 1 lime

¼ cup soy sauce

grapeseed oil

kosher salt and freshly ground pepper

1 bunch asparagus, trimmed

Method

1. In a resealable plastic bag, combine steak with garlic, chilies, lime zest, soy sauce, 2 tbsp grapeseed oil and a generous pinch of salt and pepper. Seal bag and shake around to blend ingredients and coat steak. Refrigerate for at least 30 minutes, up to 2 hours, or even overnight (in the latter case, omit the salt and add it right before grilling).

2. Toss asparagus with enough oil to coat, and a generous pinch of both salt and pepper. Remove steak from fridge and allow to come to room temperature.

3. Heat grill to high. When grill is hot, scrape any bits of marinade off the steak (season with salt if you left it out of the marinade) and place on grill. Don't touch — allow steak to cook undisturbed and develop a good crust, 6 to 7 minutes. Flip steak once and cook for a further 7 minutes on the second side for medium rare. Increase time to 8 to 9 minutes per side for medium to medium well. Remove from grill and allow to rest for 10 to 15 minutes.

4. In the meantime, place seasoned asparagus on grill and cook for 2 to 3 minutes, until the green brightens and asparagus become crisp and tender. Remove from grill.

5. Slice steak thinly and against the grain and plate up with asparagus.

Serves 4

Tip

If you're using flank steak, score one side of the steak before marinating: slice meat ⅓ of the way through in diagonal strokes first one way, then the other, to make a diamond pattern. Scoring helps this tougher cut of meat absorb the marinade and tenderize.

Sticky Sesame Chicken Wings

These are great food for a party or a really casual dinner. Roasted wings are absolutely delicious, and the fresh crunch of the sesame seeds and scallions is just perfect. This is also something kids can make really easily.

Ingredients

2 garlic cloves, minced

1½ tsp kosher salt

¼ cup soy sauce

¼ cup hoisin sauce

¼ cup honey

2 tsp sesame oil

pinch of cayenne

3 lb (1.5 kg) chicken wings, wing tips trimmed and split (about 30)

1½ tbsp sesame seeds, lightly toasted

1 scallion, green part only, finely chopped

Method

1. Place oven rack in upper third of oven and preheat oven to 425° F. Line a large, shallow baking pan with parchment paper or foil and set aside.

2. In a large bowl, combine garlic, salt, soy sauce, hoisin sauce, honey, sesame oil and cayenne. Add wings to sauce and toss well to coat.

3. Arrange wings in a single layer on baking sheet and roast, turning over once, until cooked through, about 35 minutes. If you like your wings really crisp, leave 'em in a bit longer. Remove from heat and allow to cool just slightly.

4. Transfer wings to a large serving bowl and sprinkle with sesame seeds and scallions.

Serves 4

Chicken and Guacamole Tostadas

Tostadas are crisp corn tortillas topped with any combination of meats, cheese, beans, guacamole and salsa. These tostadas can also be made on round nacho chips for an easy and delicious party food. Use refried black beans instead of chicken for a vegetarian option.

Ingredients

1 large ripe avocado, peeled, pitted

4 tsp fresh lime juice

2 green onions, chopped

1 clove garlic, minced

hot pepper sauce (such as Tabasco)

kosher salt and freshly ground pepper

2 cooked chicken breast halves, shredded (about 1¾ cups)

1 tomato, seeded, chopped

2 tbsp chopped fresh cilantro

1 tsp ground cumin

lime juice, to taste

4 tostada shells (crisp corn tortillas)

2 cups shredded lettuce

⅔ cup crumbled queso fresco or feta cheese

store-bought salsa

Method

1. To make guacamole, place avocado in medium-sized bowl. Add lime juice and mash until almost smooth. Mix in green onions and garlic. Season to taste with hot sauce, salt and pepper.

2. Combine shredded chicken, tomato, cilantro and cumin in a small bowl. Season to taste with lime juice, salt and pepper.

3. Arrange tostada shells on plates. Top with lettuce, guacamole and chicken mixture. Sprinkle with cheese. Spoon salsa over and serve.

Serves 4

Buttermilk Chive Vinaigrette

Buttermilk is a really great way to add richness to a vinaigrette without adding lots of fat, and the tart lime with the nutty tahini makes for a delicious combination.

Ingredients

¾ cup buttermilk

¼ cup lime juice

1 tsp tahini

1 clove garlic, minced

¼ cup finely chopped fresh chives

kosher salt and freshly ground pepper

¼ cup vegetable oil

Method

1. In a small bowl, whisk together all ingredients to combine. Taste and adjust seasoning as necessary. Store in an airtight container in the fridge.

Makes about 1 cup

Spice-Rubbed Chicken

This is something we make all the time for lunch, and each time it's a bit different. Use whatever spice mixture you like — have fun and experiment with flavour combinations. Serve it with Pasta Salad with Chive Pesto (page 42) for a delicious spring meal.

Ingredients

8 pieces chicken, bone in, skin on

¼ cup vegetable oil

3 cloves garlic, minced

2 tsp ground cumin

2 tsp chili powder

2 tsp dried oregano

kosher salt and freshly ground pepper

Method

1. Preheat oven to 425° F. Line a baking sheet with parchment paper and set aside. In a large mixing bowl, combine chicken pieces, oil, garlic and spices and season well with salt and pepper. Toss well to coat each piece of chicken with the spice mix.

2. Arrange chicken on baking sheet and roast for 25 to 30 minutes, until juices run clear and chicken is crispy and browned.

Serves 4

Pasta Salad with Chive Pesto

This is a springtime favourite in our kitchen. Pesto made from our garden chives ushers in the freshness of the new growing season.

Ingredients

1 lb (500 g) short pasta, like penne, fusilli or orecchiette

1½ – 2 cups chive pesto (see page 43)

1–2 tbsp extra-virgin olive oil

1 red bell pepper, seeded and finely diced

1 19-oz can (540 mL) chickpeas, drained

1 large carrot, peeled and julienned

kosher salt and freshly ground pepper

Method

1. Bring a large pot of salted water to a boil. Add pasta and cook for 10 to 12 minutes or until al dente (tender to the tooth). Drain in a colander and rinse well with cool water to stop cooking.

2. Combine cooked pasta with pesto and 1 tbsp olive oil. Mix gently to coat pasta with the pesto, adding a bit more olive oil if necessary. Add bell pepper, chickpeas and carrot and season well with salt and pepper. Toss to combine.

Serves 4 to 6

Chive Pesto

The chives are the first things we start to harvest from our garden in the spring. Making pesto is an excellent way for us to use the great quantity of chives we get — plus the flavour is fantastic.

Ingredients

2 large handfuls of chives, trimmed, flowers removed

½ cup toasted unsalted sunflower seeds

1 handful grated Parmesan cheese

juice of 1 or 2 lemons

2 cloves garlic, minced

kosher salt and freshly ground pepper

2 cups (or so) extra-virgin olive oil, or an olive-sunflower mix

Method

1. In a food processor, place chives, sunflower seeds, cheese, the juice of one lemon and garlic. Season with salt and pepper and blend until a relatively thick paste forms at the bottom of the bowl.

2. With the machine running, drizzle olive oil through the feed tube until a really nice, loose paste forms. Taste and add more salt, pepper and/or lemon juice if desired.

Makes 3 cups

Rhubarb and Sorrel Gingersnap Crumble

Rhubarb and French sorrel come up at the same time in our garden. Our garden staff excitedly brought in a bundle of bright red stalks with a bouquet of light green leaves, urging me to make a crumble. If two things are comfortable enough with each other in the ground, it's safe to say they'll be just as well matched on a plate. Feel free to omit the sorrel if you can't get your hands on any, but it adds a beautifully mysterious flavour to this delicious dessert. You can make this crumble in individual pudding dishes, as shown, if you like.

Ingredients

FILLING:
2 lb (1 kg) (6 stalks) rhubarb, trimmed and chopped into ½-inch pieces (6 cups)

1½ cups brown sugar

⅓ cup all-purpose flour

2 tsp vanilla extract

4 or 5 leaves French sorrel, torn into bite-size pieces

TOPPING:
3 cups finely ground gingersnaps

1 tsp salt

1 cup quick rolled oats

¼ cup flour

¼ cup brown sugar

1 cup cold butter, cut into small pieces, plus more for pan

Method

1. Preheat oven to 375°F. Butter a 9- x 13-inch baking pan or casserole dish and set aside.

2. Make filling: in a large bowl, combine rhubarb, brown sugar, flour, vanilla and sorrel and toss well to mix.

3. Make topping: in a medium-sized mixing bowl, combine gingersnaps, salt, oats, flour and brown sugar and stir. Add butter and, using your fingertips, incorporate it into the dry mixture until you have pea-size pieces.

4. Transfer rhubarb mixture to prepared pan and press down slightly to pack it in. Sprinkle crumble topping over rhubarb in an even layer and bake for 30 to 40 minutes, or until top is browned and rhubarb starts to bubble on the sides of the pan. Remove from heat and allow to cool slightly. Serve warm with vanilla ice cream.

Serves 6 to 8

Seasonal Notes
Here are some seasonal substitutes for rhubarb (use the same weight of fruit):

Summer: peach & blueberry, nectarine & blackberry
Fall: pear, plum **Winter:** apple

Rhubarb-ade

This recipe came from our Urban Agriculture staff as the perfect beverage for our garden's 10th birthday party. It's an ideal way to use rhubarb and mint, two things in great abundance in many gardens. You can freeze the concentrate as well as substitute any kind of sweetener you wish for the maple syrup. While rhubarb is beautifully sour, it's missing some brightness, which is why we added a bit of lemon juice to the mix.

Ingredients

6–7 cups chopped rhubarb

1 cup maple syrup

juice of 1 lemon (optional)

water

handful of fresh mint leaves

Method

1. In a medium-sized sauce pan, combine rhubarb and maple syrup. Fill with water to just above the level of the rhubarb and bring to a boil. Reduce heat slightly and continue boiling rhubarb until very mushy, about 10 minutes.

2. Remove from heat and pass mixture through a fine mesh sieve, using a wooden spoon or spatula to really press the mixture through. Pour this concentrate into a pitcher and add lemon juice. Add water, 1 to 2 cups at a time, to dilute, tasting as you go. Cut the sourness with more maple syrup if necessary.

3. Tear or bruise the mint leaves with your hands (to release the flavour) and add to pitcher. Stir to combine and refrigerate for a couple of hours to chill completely.

Makes one pitcher

Banana Bread with Flaxseed

Overripe bananas are crying out to be turned into banana bread. This version has flaxseeds, whole wheat flour and walnuts, which really boost the nutrition.

Ingredients

2 tbsp unsalted butter, melted, plus 1 teaspoon, softened, for pan

½ cup whole wheat flour

¾ cup all-purpose flour

¼ cup flaxseeds

¾ tsp salt

½ tsp baking powder

½ tsp baking soda

1 large egg plus 1 large egg white

½ cup brown sugar

1½ tsp vanilla extract

¾ cup mashed very ripe bananas (about 2 medium bananas)

½ cup toasted and coarsely chopped walnuts

Method

1. Preheat oven to 350° F. Butter a 9- x 5- x 3-inch loaf pan and set aside. In a medium-sized bowl, whisk together the flours, flaxseeds, salt, baking powder and baking soda and set aside.

2. Put egg and egg white in the bowl of an electric mixer fitted with the paddle attachment, and mix on medium-low speed until well combined, about 2 minutes. (If you don't have a stand mixer, you can easily do this in a mixing bowl with a whisk). Add melted butter, sugar, vanilla and bananas, and mix until combined. Add reserved flour mixture and mix on low speed (or switch to a spatula if mixing by hand) until well incorporated, about 10 seconds. Stir in walnuts.

3. Pour batter into buttered pan. Bake until bread is golden brown and a wooden toothpick inserted into the centre comes out clean, about 45 to 50 minutes. Let cool slightly in pan on a wire rack. Invert bread to unmold; reinvert and let cool completely on rack.

Makes 1 loaf

Tips

• You can substitute spelt flour for both the all-purpose and whole wheat flours.

• Freezing very ripe bananas works really well... just make a note on the package how many bananas' worth are inside and make sure you thaw them completely before you use them.

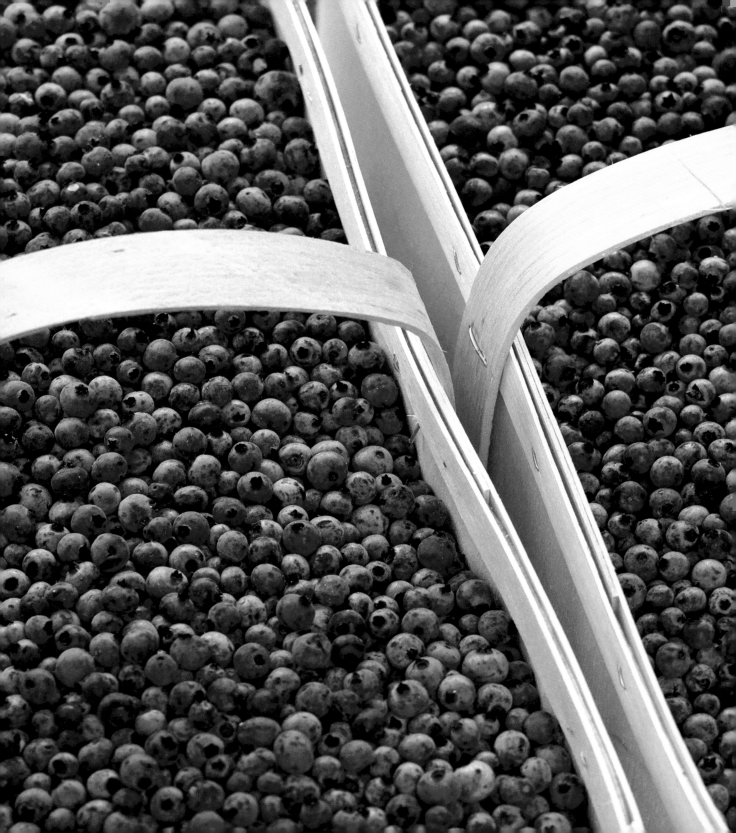

beans apricots
blueberries broccoli
carrots cauliflower
cherries nectarines
sweet corn peaches
cucumber summer
lettuce mushrooms
watermelon pears
onions raspberries
snow peas zucchini
spinach tomatoes
gooseberries

Summer Preserves

In summer, The Stop's gardens are a hive of activity, and The Green Barn farmers' market kicks into full swing. Our cooks make sure they have stacks of Mason jars at the ready to preserve as many fruits and vegetables as they can. Our volunteers go on trips to farms outside the city, where they can hand-pick the last of the fruit. For many, it's their only trip out of the city all year long.

Later on, some of the gleaners join our cooks at the popular preserving workshops. Buying local strawberries at the peak of the season to make freezer jam (page 75) just makes sense: not only do the local berries cost less than fruit out of season, they taste far better than anything California sends us through the winter.

As more and more produce arrives from the garden, we struggle to keep up: summer squash, snow peas, cherry tomatoes, you name it. We used to pull up callaloo, which we thought was inedible, until Herman Plunkett, a Jamaican-Canadian neighbour and self-appointed guardian of the garden, caught us in the act. He showed our staff how his family used to cook the nutritious green for Sunday lunch; now it has a place of honour in the garden. It's also a popular item at The Stop's food bank because it's so expensive and hard to find in stores.

Just-picked greens, fairly vibrating with life, arrive in a wooden crate...

There are always surprises, like the generous donations from our community neighbours. Just-picked greens, fairly vibrating with life, arrive in a wooden crate from a volunteer at the Church of the Redeemer. Our gardeners might bring us an unexpected harvest of zucchini blossoms — a delicacy that most of our community members could never afford. When the blossoms arrive in the kitchen, our Italian volunteers stare at them in disbelief. Soon everyone is battering them up to make fritters for lunch.

The more you cook, the more flexible you can be in the kitchen. At The Stop, the old adage "waste not, want not" is put into practice daily: even Swiss chard stems can be braised with a little garlic, olive oil and water to serve as a side dish. And veggie trimmings that can't be eaten go back into the compost to feed the garden soil.

On pizza night, when our centre is filled with people young and old, immigrants and native Torontonians, staff and volunteers, donors and beneficiaries, it's easy to find more similarities than differences among us. Everybody loves the pizzas (page 68) that come out of the wood-fired brick oven. Each pie is unique — topped according to the taste of the maker, with pepperoni, mozzarella, a few veggies from the garden — but all of them fulfill the same purpose: to feed our bellies, hearts and minds. –S.C.

Peach Salsa

The glory of salsa is the way it introduces so many different flavours into your mouth at once. Spend the time to chop everything finely, and you'll be rewarded with a delicious and complex mouthful. Feel free to substitute virtually any fruit for the peaches. We've tried everything from watermelon and plum to papaya with great success.

Ingredients

4 ripe peaches, peeled, pitted and finely diced

1 small white onion, very finely diced

1 small handful fresh cilantro, finely chopped

1 jalapeno, finely minced (or to taste)

juice of 1 or 2 limes

1 tbsp vegetable oil

kosher salt and freshly ground pepper

Method

1. Combine diced peaches, onion, cilantro and jalapeno in a small mixing bowl. Add juice of 1 lime, vegetable oil and season well with salt and pepper. Stir to combine and taste. Add more lime juice, salt or pepper as necessary. Allow to sit for 10 minutes before serving.

Makes about 2 cups

Stop Staff Salad

This is a very common lunch among our staff. Everyone shows up with a little something to contribute, and before long we have a hearty and healthy meal that is shared during a welcome break in our busy workday. The recipe here is the most common incarnation of this salad, but it's really about using whatever you have available.

Ingredients

5 large handfuls salad greens, washed, dried and torn into bite-size pieces

⅓ English cucumber, chopped

2 tomatoes, chopped

1 ripe avocado, peeled, pitted and roughly chopped

1 small handful sprouts

1 19-oz (540 mL) can chickpeas, drained

1 small handful dried cranberries

1 small handful sliced almonds, toasted

½ cup extra-virgin olive oil

¼ cup balsamic vinegar

kosher salt and freshly ground pepper

Method

1. In a large salad bowl, combine greens, cucumber, tomatoes, avocado, sprouts and chickpeas; sprinkle cranberries and almonds over top.

2. In a small bowl, whisk together oil and vinegar, and season with salt and pepper. Pour 2/3 dressing over salad and toss well to coat. Taste and add additional dressing as necessary.

Serves 6 to 8

Za'atar Chicken Burgers with Minted Yogurt

Za'atar is the Middle Eastern spice mix that gives these burgers their distinctive flavour. See the recipe on page 58 for our version. We make a mini size and serve them on whole wheat dinner rolls.

Ingredients

2 lb (1 kg) lean ground chicken

1 small onion, finely diced

3 cloves garlic, minced

1 small handful fresh parsley, finely chopped

2 eggs

⅓ – ½ cup bread crumbs

kosher salt and freshly ground pepper

2 tbsp za'atar (page 58)

16 mini-burger buns (or dinner rolls)

1 cup Balkan-style yogurt, strained (see tip)

¼ cup finely chopped fresh mint

juice of ½ lemon

1 pkg onion sprouts (about 1 cup)

Method

1. In a large mixing bowl, combine chicken, onion, garlic, parsley, eggs, 1/3 cup breadcrumbs and za'atar; season well with salt and pepper. Using your hands, mix well, to thoroughly combine ingredients, adding more breadcrumbs if necessary.

2. Form mixture into patties about 2 inches in diameter, or just larger than the buns.

3. Preheat grill pan to high. Grill burgers 1 to 2 minutes per side, or until nicely browned outside and cooked through. Remove from heat and set aside.

4. In a small mixing bowl, combine strained yogurt, mint and lemon juice. Season with salt and pepper and stir well.

5. Slice each bun in half and place a burger on bottom half. Smear a bit of the yogurt mixture on top, garnish with a tablespoon of onion sprouts and cap with top half of bun.

Makes about 16 mini-burgers

Tip

To strain yogurt: line a bowl with a piece of cheesecloth. Pour the yogurt into the cheesecloth-lined bowl and gather up all four corners of the cloth. Hang the yogurt off the faucet of your sink for 2 hours, or even overnight for a very rich yogurt cheese. For a quicker version, place a fine mesh sieve on the rim of a mixing bowl and pour yogurt into sieve. Allow to sit for at least one hour before using.

Za'atar

This spice blend is incredibly versatile — it can be used in salads, dips and soups, and as a rub for meats.

Ingredients

¼ cup sesame seeds

2 tbsp dried thyme

2 tbsp dried oregano

¼ cup ground sumac

2 tsp kosher salt

Method

1. Preheat oven to 350° F. Sprinkle the sesame seeds on a baking sheet and toast in oven for 5 to 7 minutes, or until lightly browned and fragrant. Remove from heat and set aside to cool.

2. Combine thyme, oregano and sumac in small bowl. Add sesame seeds and salt and stir to mix.

3. Store in an airtight container in a cool, dark place.

Makes 1 cup

Roasted Potato Salad with Herbed Buttermilk Dressing

We have made this salad for many meals and events at The Stop, and we always run out. Roasting the potatoes gives the dish a crispy edge, which perfectly complements the generous helping of fresh herbs. Use any potatoes you like — we've even made a successful version with sweet potatoes. This dish is pictured with the Marinated Flank Steak on page 61.

Ingredients

¾ cup mayonnaise

⅓ cup buttermilk

3 tbsp Dijon mustard

2 tbsp fresh lemon juice

2 tsp apple cider vinegar

2 cloves garlic, minced

kosher salt and freshly ground pepper

2 lb (1 kg) small red-skinned potatoes, cut into halves

3 tbsp extra-virgin olive oil

1 large handful each dill, parsley, scallions, chopped finely

Method

1. Preheat oven to 425° F. In a medium-sized bowl, whisk together mayonnaise, buttermilk, mustard, lemon juice, vinegar and garlic until blended. Season to taste with salt and pepper. Set aside.

2. In a large bowl, toss potatoes with olive oil and season well with salt and pepper. Arrange in a single layer on a parchment-lined baking sheet and roast for 30 minutes, or until browned and crispy. Remove from heat and let cool.

3. In a large bowl, combine roasted potatoes, herbs, scallions and 1/2 the buttermilk dressing, toss gently to combine. Taste and add more dressing in small amounts until potatoes are well coated.

Serves 4 to 6

Marinated Flank Steak

This is a very flavourful steak and tastes best when it's cut into thin slices. Flank steak is a delicious cut of meat that doesn't get enough credit, simply because it's a bit tougher than other more popular cuts. This marinade has lots of acid, which will tenderize the meat beautifully.

Ingredients

1 flank steak, about 1½ lbs (750g), well trimmed

2 tbsp low-sodium soy sauce

3 garlic cloves, minced

1 or 2 sprigs fresh rosemary

2 fresh red chilies, split lengthwise, or 1 tbsp dried crushed chilies

2 or 3 sprigs fresh thyme

2 teaspoons extra-virgin olive oil

kosher salt and freshly ground pepper

Method

1. Using a sharp knife, score the steak at 1-inch intervals, cutting 1/3 of the way into the meat (take care not to cut all the way through). Combine soy sauce, garlic, rosemary, chilies, thyme and oil in a resealable plastic bag and add steak. Season generously with pepper. Squeezing air out, seal bag and toss around, massaging marinade into meat. Lay bag in a 9- x 13-inch pan and refrigerate at least 30 minutes, turning occasionally.

2. Heat grill on high until almost smoking. Remove steak from bag and wipe off any bits of marinade. Season generously with salt and place on grill, scored side down. (You should hear the sizzle as the meat makes contact with the grill; if you don't, your grill is not hot enough.)

3. Allow steak to cook undisturbed to develop a good crust, 6 to 7 minutes. Flip and cook for a further 6 to 7 minutes on the other side for medium rare. (Increase time by a minute or two for medium or medium-well steak.) Remove from grill and let rest for 10 minutes.

4. Slice thinly across the grain and serve.

Serves 4

Stuffed Swiss Chard Leaves

This is a variation on Middle Eastern stuffed grapevine leaves, and it's a really easy thing to make considering how delicious it is to eat. You can use rice or couscous instead of bulgur, and adding some ground beef to the onion mixture is quite delicious too. Although we often associate Swiss chard with winter, it's available nearly year-round.

Ingredients

1 lb (500 kg) Swiss chard, stalks carefully removed

½ cup orange juice

½ cup water

1 cup bulgur

1 tbsp extra-virgin olive oil

½ medium onion, finely diced

3 cloves of garlic, minced

3 medium tomatoes, seeded and finely diced

¼ tsp ground cumin

pinch of cinnamon

pinch of allspice

1 handful chives, finely chopped

¼ cup very finely chopped fresh mint

1 lemon, cut into wedges

kosher salt and freshly ground pepper

Method

1. Bring a medium-sized pot of salted water to a boil. Keep a bowl of ice water nearby. Blanch Swiss chard for exactly 30 seconds, then drain immediately and plunge into ice water to stop cooking. Once cool, remove from water and pat dry.

2. In a small saucepan, combine orange juice and water and bring to a boil. Place bulgur in a medium-sized bowl. Pour juice mixture over the bulgur, season with salt and pepper, stir and cover with plastic wrap. Set aside for 20 minutes.

3. Heat olive oil in a sauté pan over medium-high heat. Add onion, season lightly with salt and pepper and cook until translucent. Add garlic, tomatoes, cumin, cinnamon and allspice; season with salt and pepper and sauté just until tomatoes are slightly softened and mixture is fragrant.

4. Once the bulgur has cooled sufficiently, fluff it with a fork. Add tomato spice mixture and stir gently to incorporate. Finally, add chives and mint and season lightly once more with salt and pepper. Toss to combine.

6. Lay one of the blanched chard leaves on a cutting board. Slice lengthwise down the middle of the leaf to make two roughly even pieces. Turn each piece horizontally, and place a 3-inch sausage of bulgur mixture in the centre of it. Fold the sides over each other towards the centre, then roll up like a cigar and place seam side down in a serving dish. Repeat with remaining leaves and filling. Serve with a squeeze of fresh lemon juice.

Makes 12 to 16 rolls

Apricot and Brown Rice Pilaf

Sautéeing the onions and coriander first helps to build great flavour in the pan, which will infuse the nutty brown rice. Feel free to substitute vegetable broth or stock for chicken, and almonds or pumpkin seeds for the hazelnuts. This dish is pictured with the Seared Rainbow Trout with Greens on page 65.

Ingredients

1 tbsp butter

1 small onion, minced

¼ tsp ground coriander

kosher salt and freshly ground pepper

1 cup long grain brown rice

2 cups chicken broth or stock

½ cup chopped apricots (in ½-inch pieces)

2 tbsp chopped flat-leaf parsley

¼ cup toasted and roughly chopped hazelnuts (optional)

Method

1. In a medium saucepan, melt butter over medium heat. Cook onion, stirring occasionally, until golden brown, about 8 minutes.

2. Add coriander and season with salt and pepper. Add rice; cook, stirring, until edges are transparent, about 2 minutes.

3. Stir in chicken stock and add apricots. Bring to a boil. Cover; simmer over low heat until liquid is absorbed, about 40 minutes. Remove from heat; let stand, covered, 10 minutes.

4. Stir parsley into rice gently with a fork. Sprinkle with hazelnuts, if using, and serve.

Serves 4 to 6

Seared Rainbow Trout with Greens

Virtually any fish will do well with these flavours. Use as fresh and local a fish as you can get your hands on. This recipe came from one of our cooking classes and was a huge hit! Delicious served with greens, brown rice pilaf and lemon slices.

Ingredients

4 6-oz (170 g) rainbow trout fillets, cleaned

grapeseed or canola oil

kosher salt and freshly ground pepper

1 bunch Swiss chard, washed, ribs removed and leaves roughly torn

2 lemons

Method

1. Preheat oven to 425° F. Rub fish with enough oil to thinly coat, and season well with salt and pepper. Heat a non-stick skillet on high until pan is very hot. Place fish, flesh side down in pan and sear until a nice browned crust is formed but the fish is not fully cooked through. The fish will release itself once crust is formed. Turn fish and sear second side, just long enough to build another good crust. Transfer fish to a baking sheet and continue cooking in oven until just done, about 3 to 5 minutes more. Fish should be flaky and moist.

2. Heat a large sauté pan on high heat. Add 1 tablespoon grapeseed oil and swirl to coat pan. Add chard and season with salt and pepper. Using tongs, toss chard around in pan until bright green and just wilted. Remove from heat and squeeze with juice of 1/2 a lemon. Serve immediately.

Serves 4

Fish Tacos

These are incredibly quick and easy to make. Use the freshest fish available to you, and feel free to substitute shrimp or any other kind of seafood you like. The fruit salsa pairs beautifully with fish, and cabbage adds a nice fresh crunch. Tacos are so simple, but so satisfying.

Ingredients

1 lb (500 g) white fish fillets (tilapia, cod, etc.)

vegetable oil

kosher salt and freshly ground pepper

2 limes

1 cup sour cream

1 ½ cups shredded green or napa cabbage

8–12 small corn tortillas

peach salsa (see page 54)

Method

1. Preheat broiler. Rub fish with a teaspoon of vegetable oil and season well with salt and pepper. Lay fish on baking sheet lined with parchment paper and broil until opaque and just cooked through, 4 to 5 minutes, depending on the thickness. Remove from heat and allow to cool.

2. In a small bowl, combine zest of 1 lime with sour cream. Set aside. Using two forks, gently flake fish apart to produce 1-inch pieces. Place in a bowl and set aside.

3. Squeeze juice from the zested lime over the shredded cabbage, season lightly with salt and pepper, and toss gently to combine. Cut remaining lime into wedges and set aside.

4. Heat a dry skillet to medium high and toast two tortillas at a time, flipping occasionally to warm through. If not serving immediately, stack and wrap loosely in foil.

5. Assemble tacos with some fish, cabbage, peach salsa and a dollop of lime sour cream. Serve with lime wedges.

Serves 4

Our Bake Oven Pizza Dough

For years now, we've been making pizzas in the bake oven behind our community centre. With fresh produce from the garden, each pizza is elevated to a thing of beauty. You'll want to get started on the dough the day before so it has time to rise. This dough also freezes beautifully; just be sure to let it come to room temperature before using.

Ingredients

1½ tbsp active dry yeast

2¼ cups warm water

½ tbsp sugar

2 tsp salt

2½ cups all-purpose flour

2½ cups whole wheat flour

2 tbsp vegetable or olive oil

2 tbsp vegetable or olive oil (for bowl)

cornmeal for baking sheet

Method

1. In a mixing bowl, combine yeast, warm water, sugar and salt. Stir and set aside for about 10 minutes to dissolve and activate yeast. Combine flours in a bowl and set aside.

2. Place yeast mixture in the bowl of an electric mixer fitted with the dough hook attachment. With the mixer on low, gradually add flour until dough is mixed well. Increase speed to medium high and knead for about 4 to 6 minutes. The dough should be homogenous, smooth and all collected around the hook. Place the dough in a large oiled bowl, cover loosely with plastic wrap and refrigerate to rise overnight.

3. Next day punch down dough, allow to come to room temperature and roll into balls about the size of a lemon for individual pizzas, or 3 big balls for large pizzas. Arrange dough balls on an oiled baking tray with a bit of space between them and cover with a kitchen towel. Leave in a warm place for about 30 minutes to rise again.

4. Preheat oven to 500° F. If using a pizza stone, place it in the oven to heat up; otherwise, sprinkle cornmeal generously on an inverted baking sheet. Using your hands and a rolling pin, stretch and roll out dough to make 8-inch rounds for individual pizzas, or whatever size you wish. Place dough on inverted, cornmeal-sprinkled baking sheet or pizza peel and garnish with sauce, veggies and cheese as desired. Use peel to transfer pizzas to stone, or place upturned baking sheet in oven. Bake pizzas for about 8 to 10 minutes, or until nicely browned and cheese is bubbling.

Makes 12 individual pizzas, or 3 large ones

Tip

If you don't have a rimless baking sheet, turn a rimmed baking sheet upside down to allow the baked pizza to slide off easily.

Classic Crêpes

This is an easy recipe for crêpes. Fill them with anything — fresh fruit, ham and cheese, Nutella or whipped cream. For savoury crêpes, you can add fresh herbs and more salt and pepper to the batter, A crêpe pan and an offset spatula (one with a bend in the blade) make the job much easier, but you can achieve the same results with a regular, non-stick skillet and an egg flipper. Just remember to go easy on the greasing, and to get the pan swirling the second the batter hits it. See chart on page 72 for sweet and savoury filling suggestions.

Ingredients

½ cup all-purpose flour

pinch of salt

2 large eggs

1 large egg yolk

1¼ cups milk

1½ tsp vanilla extract

6 tbsp unsalted butter, melted and cooled

vegetable oil for frying

Method

1. In a medium-sized bowl, sift together flour and salt. Whisk in eggs, egg yolk, and about 1 tablespoon milk, to make a smooth batter with a paste-like consistency.

2. Add remaining milk and 1 teaspoon vanilla; mix until no lumps remain. Add melted butter and whisk to combine. Let the batter rest at room temperature about 30 minutes.

3. Heat oven to warm. Over medium-low heat, warm a crêpe pan or non-stick skillet thoroughly. Using a pastry brush, brush pan with a very thin coating of oil, making sure there is not enough oil to pool in the corners when you rotate the pan. Stir batter, take pan off heat and carefully ladle about 1/4 cup batter into skillet. Rotate skillet so batter spreads out and thinly coats the bottom and edges of the skillet. You will have to do a few trial runs to get the perfect pan temperature and batter quantity.

4. Return pan to heat and cook crêpe until edges turn golden brown and lacy, and start to pull away from the pan, about 2 minutes. Using your fingers or an offset spatula, carefully turn crêpe over; cook other side until just golden, 30 to 40 seconds. Slide the crêpe onto a heat-proof plate, cover loosely with aluminum foil and place in the oven to keep warm. Repeat with the remaining batter, stirring it before making each crêpe. Stack cooked crêpes on plate as you go, returning it to the oven after each addition.

Serves 4

Here are some suggestions for sweet and savoury crêpe fillings. Quantities are enough for 4 crêpes, unless otherwise specified.

Filling	Method
apples (or pears) with maple cream	Peel, core and slice 2 apples into ½-inch slices. Heat 2 tbsp butter in a sauté pan to medium-high heat. Sauté apples, adding 2 tbsp maple syrup and ½ tsp cinnamon, until apples are tender but still a bit crisp. Whip 1 cup heavy cream, adding 1 tbsp maple syrup halfway through. Divide apple mixture among crêpes, fold and top with a dollop of whipped cream.
Nutella and bananas	Slice 2 ripe bananas into ½-inch slices. Spread 2 tbsp Nutella on each crêpe, arrange a half-banana's worth of slices on top and fold.
balsamic strawberries	Slice tops off 2 cups strawberries. Slice berries and place in a small bowl. Drizzle 2 tbsp balsamic vinegar over strawberries and toss gently to combine. Divide mixture among crêpes and fold.
herb and lemon	Add ¼ cup finely chopped fresh herbs to batter. Slice 1 lemon into wedges and sprinkle folded herb crêpes with lemon juice.
ham/turkey and cheddar/Swiss	Lay 2 slices deli ham or turkey on each crêpe and sprinkle with ¼ cup grated cheddar or Swiss cheese. Fold and keep cooking to just melt cheese.
curried mayonnaise with chicken and scallion	Combine ½ cup mayonnaise with 1 tsp curry powder and season with salt and pepper. Slice 2 scallions very thinly, and shred 2 cups cooked chicken with two forks. Spread 1 tbsp curried mayonnaise on each crêpe. Sprinkle each crêpe with ½ cup shredded chicken and ¼ of the scallions and fold.
portobello with goat cheese	Marinate 2 portobello mushrooms in ¼ cup olive oil, 2 tbsp balsamic vinegar, salt and pepper. Grill mushrooms on high until tender and crisp; remove from heat and slice thinly. Divide mushrooms between crêpes, crumble 2 tbsp goat cheese and sprinkle 1 sprig's worth of fresh thyme leaves onto each crêpe and fold.
fried egg and Swiss cheese	At step 4 of crêpe directions, before edges become crisp and lacy, crack 1 egg onto each crêpe and season with salt and pepper. Cook until egg is done to your liking. Sprinkle with ¼ cup grated Swiss cheese, fold and continue cooking to melt cheese, taking care not to let crêpe burn.

Spelt Oat Crêpes

To celebrate Mother's Day, our Healthy Beginnings breakfast program held a Crêpe-Off, with the classic crêpe (see page 70) going toe to toe against this more wholesome version. The verdict? The healthy crêpes are surprisingly delicious, as well as a great way to get some of the goodness of oats and spelt.

Ingredients

¾ cup spelt flour

¾ cup quick rolled oats

2 cups soy milk

1 tbsp vegetable oil, plus more for pan

1 tsp salt

Method

1. Make batter: Combine flour, oats, soy milk, 1 tablespoon oil and salt in a blender and blend until smooth. Transfer to a bowl and let rest at room temperature for 10 minutes.

2. Cook crêpes: Heat oven to warm. Over medium-low heat, warm a crêpe pan or non-stick skillet thoroughly. Using a pastry brush, brush pan with a thin coating of oil, making sure there is not enough oil to pool in the corners when you rotate the pan. Stir batter, take pan off heat and carefully ladle about 1/4 cup batter into pan. Rotate pan so batter spreads out and thinly coats the bottom and edges of the pan. You will have to do a few trial runs to get the perfect pan temperature and batter quantity.

3. Return pan to heat and cook crêpe until edges turn golden brown and lacy and start to pull away from the pan, about 2 minutes. Using your fingers or an offset spatula, carefully turn crêpe over; cook other side until just golden, 30 to 40 seconds. Slide the crêpe onto a heat-proof plate, loosely cover with aluminum foil and place in the oven to keep warm. Repeat with the remaining batter, stirring it before making each crêpe. Stack cooked crêpes on plate as you go, returning it to the oven after each addition.

Serves 12

Blueberry Spelt Pancakes

These are a favourite in our community kitchens, and we think that the spelt actually makes them much better than the white-flour originals. You can replace the blueberries with bananas, pears or other berries.

Ingredients

1 cup spelt flour

1½ tsp baking powder

pinch of salt

⅔ cup milk

1 egg, lightly beaten

butter, for frying

1 cup fresh blueberries

Method

1. Combine flour, baking powder and salt in a mixing bowl. In another bowl, combine milk and egg. Add liquid ingredients to dry and whisk together until just combined (lumps are okay!).

2. In a non-stick frying pan, melt a teaspoon of butter on medium heat until frothy. Pour 2 to 3 tablespoons of batter into the pan and allow to spread. Cook for 1 to 2 minutes, then scatter a small handful of blueberries on top (there should be bubbles on the surface). Flip and cook for another minute. Repeat with remaining batter, adding more butter to the pan as necessary. Serve hot with maple syrup.

Makes about 6

Flour	How to Use
all-purpose	As its name suggests, this refined white flour can be used for almost anything, from breads to cakes, pastries and cookies.
whole wheat	This is a harder flour that is more wholesome, has less gluten, and works best when paired with some all-purpose flour; you can successfully substitute whole wheat flour for ½ your total flour requirement, but make sure you use some all-purpose flour to balance it out.
cake and pastry	This softer flour helps make delicate things like cakes and pastries light and airy.
spelt	This ancient grain is higher in protein than wheat and digests more easily; you can substitute it for wheat in most recipes, excluding some lighter cakes and pastries.
rice, potato	These flours have no gluten and are perfect for crumbly baked goods like shortbread or tart crusts.

Easy Strawberry Freezer Jam

We held a jam-making workshop after a day of picking strawberries and tried both cooked and freezer jam recipes. While both were delicious, the bright freshness that is preserved with the uncooked method was the hands-down winner — and we now make only freezer jam.

Ingredients

10 cups strawberries, hulled, washed and chopped into quarters

2 cups granulated sugar

2 pkg (1½ oz/45 g each) freezer jam pectin (any brand will do)

Method

1. Sterilize 5 x 16-oz (500 mL) preserving jars and lids and set aside.

2. Place strawberries in a bowl and mash well, until pulpy and liquidy.

3. Add sugar and pectin and stir well for 2 to 3 minutes to dissolve. Taste and adjust sweetness if necessary. Allow to sit for 5 minutes or so to make sure pectin and sugar are completely dissolved and incorporated.

4. Fill bottles to just below the neck with jam, cover and freeze for up to 8 months. Once jam has been thawed, it can be stored in the fridge for up to 2 months.

Makes 5 500 mL jars

The Easiest Peach Ice Cream

This recipe is almost too good to be true — frozen peaches and a food processor produce a perfect ice cream that doesn't need to be churned. Use absolutely any fruit you like, as long as it's frozen. And for the best results, fill the food processor only half full. This is a deliciously wholesome way to enjoy fruit... and in just a few minutes!

Ingredients

2 cups frozen peaches

½ cup yogurt

1–2 tbsp maple syrup

½ tsp cinnamon

Method

1. Combine all ingredients in the bowl of a food processor and blend until smooth. Serve immediately, or scrape into a plastic container and freeze.

Makes about 1 litre

Oatmeal Zucchini Loaf

This is a hearty, healthful bread that we make for breakfast at our Drop-in. Turbinado sugar is a coarse, unrefined sugar that adds a sweet crunch to the crust... it won't make or break the loaf, so don't sweat it if you don't have any. This recipe is a perfect way to use up all that zucchini from the garden — and feel free to experiment with different grains, nuts and dried fruit.

Ingredients

1½ cups all-purpose flour

1 cup whole wheat flour

1 cup quick rolled oats

1 tsp baking powder

¾ tsp salt

½ tsp baking soda

3 eggs

1⅓ cups brown sugar

1 cup unsweetened applesauce

¼ cup butter, melted

1 tsp vanilla extract

2 cups shredded, unpeeled zucchini

1 cup chopped pecans

¾ cup dried cranberries

turbinado sugar, for sprinkling

Method

1. Preheat oven to 350° F. Lightly coat a 9- x 5- x 3-inch loaf pan with baking spray; set aside. In a medium-sized bowl, combine the flours, oats, baking powder, salt and baking soda; set aside.

2. In a large mixing bowl, whisk eggs for 2 minutes or until foamy. Add brown sugar, applesauce, butter and vanilla. Gradually add the flour mixture, stirring just until combined. Fold in zucchini, nuts and dried fruit. Pour into prepared pan and sprinkle with turbinado sugar.

3. Bake for 1 hour and 20 minutes or until a wooden toothpick inserted near the centre comes out clean. Cool in pan on wire rack for 10 minutes. Remove from pan and cool completely on rack.

Makes one loaf

Stop Cookies

We made these cookies the first time for our harvest festival last year, and they were such a hit, we decided to make the recipe a house specialty. These are hearty, delicious cookies that are also wholesome. People will follow their noses into the kitchen!

Ingredients

1 cup (2 sticks) unsalted butter, at room temperature

2 cups packed brown sugar

2 large eggs, at room temperature

1 tsp vanilla extract

3 cups old-fashioned rolled oats

1 cup spelt flour

½ cup wheat germ

1 tsp baking soda

1 tsp baking powder

1½ cups mixed dried fruits and nuts (such as golden raisins, currants, coarsely chopped dried apricots, dried cherries, coarsely chopped pecans, chocolate chips)

Method

1. In the bowl of an electric mixer fitted with the paddle attachment, cream butter and brown sugar on medium speed until light and fluffy, about 3 minutes (you can also do this with a spatula in a large mixing bowl). Add eggs; mix on high speed to combine. Stir in vanilla; set aside.

2. In a large bowl, combine oats, flour, wheat germ, baking soda and baking powder. Add flour mixture to butter mixture and beat on low speed to combine, 10 to 15 seconds. Remove bowl from mixer and stir in dried fruits and nuts. Refrigerate for at least 30 minutes, until firm.

3. Line baking sheets with parchment paper. Drop tablespoonfuls (or use an ice cream scoop) of dough onto prepared sheets, about 2 inches apart. Freeze until totally firm.

4. Preheat oven to 350° F. Bake frozen cookie dough until golden and just set, about 18 minutes (less time if using a convection oven). Transfer sheets to wire rack to cool.

Makes about 3 dozen

Community

A stranger arrives in a village, hungry, but the locals think they can't spare any food. The village isn't so much a community as a collection of inhabitants — people are as wary of each other as they are of newcomers. So the stranger announces he will make a soup out of stones and water. The villagers, curious to know how this can be done, come to watch; before they realize it, they are contributing their own vegetables and spices to season the broth. In the end, the entire village sits down to eat the meal — which is now a banquet — the meal that began so humbly with a few stones and some water.

Nearly every culture has a variation on this folktale. But however ancient it may be, the tale seems especially poignant today in a multicultural city like Toronto, where so many newcomers don't have the comfort of an established network or community, and even people who grew up here can feel isolated and alone.

Every meal we put together at The Stop feels a little like a retelling of that tale. It's always a collaboration between staff, community members and volunteers — some of them former participants. Food, whether it's a simple snack laid out on the table at a workshop or a hot lunch prepared by a visiting celebrity chef, changes the dynamic of our drop-in centre. No matter how tough things get, everyone feels better when they have broken bread together.

At The Stop, food is an end in itself. Hungry bellies must be fed before you can get down to the business of tackling the other challenges facing our community members, such as trying to navigate the byzantine immigration process or escaping an abusive partner. But it's also a means to an end: when people work together in a garden, cook together in the kitchen and sit down together for a meal, it helps to create bridges, break down isolation, and chip away at prejudice and indifference. *-S.C.*

Healthy Strawberry Bread with Vanilla Mascarpone

This is a delicious alternative to banana or carrot quickbreads. Strawberries add a lovely fresh flavour, while the rich mascarpone is just indulgent enough.

Ingredients

5 tbsp plus 1 tsp unsalted butter, softened, plus more for pan

1 pint strawberries, rinsed, hulled, quartered and mashed with a fork

1½ cups spelt flour

¼ cup wheat germ

1 tsp baking soda

½ tsp ground cinnamon

¼ tsp baking powder

¼ tsp salt

1 cup sugar

2 large eggs

⅓ cup milk

1 cup mascarpone cheese, at room temperature

1 vanilla bean, scraped or 2 tsp vanilla extract

¼ cup icing sugar

Method

1. Preheat oven to 350° F. Butter an 8- x 4-inch loaf pan. In a small saucepan, bring strawberries to a boil over medium heat. Cook, stirring, for 1 minute. Set aside.

2. In a medium-sized bowl, whisk together flour, wheat germ, baking soda, cinnamon, baking powder and salt; set aside. With an electric mixer, cream butter, sugar and eggs in a mixing bowl until light and fluffy. With mixer running, add flour mixture alternately with milk, beginning and ending with flour. Fold in reserved strawberries.

3. Scrape batter into prepared pan, smoothing top. Bake until a wooden toothpick inserted in centre comes out clean, about 1 hour (tent with foil after 45 minutes if top is getting too dark). Cool in pan 10 minutes. Run a knife around edges; invert onto a rack. Reinvert; cool completely.

4. Combine mascarpone, vanilla seeds and icing sugar in a small mixing bowl and stir well to combine. Slice loaf and serve with a dollop of mascarpone mixture.

Serves 8 to 10

A Note about Vanilla Beans

Vanilla beans are actually the fruit of the orchid. There are thousands of varieties, but only the apple green—coloured orchid produces anything edible. Curing the pods for 3 to 6 months after picking creates that distinctive sweet taste and fragrance. Each bean contains countless flavour-packed seeds, which are scraped out and added to cooking. Scraped vanilla pods in your sugar jar will infuse the sugar with wonderful aroma.

brussels sprouts
swiss chard apples
cauliflower carrots
celery pears beans
pumpkin garlic
grapes rapini fall
rutabaga eggplant
leeks winter squash
broccoli peaches
tomatoes beets

Fall Harvest

What do you do when a gardener arrives at your doorstep with a wheelbarrowful of green tomatoes? Make Green Tomato Ketchup (page 110), of course! The Stop's kitchen, although big enough to make lunch for 200, doesn't have tons of bells and whistles. What we do have is a steady stream of willing volunteers. Everyone joins in: even kids stand on milk crates so they can reach the giant wooden spoons. It helps that the green ketchup looks like some sort of witches' brew.

Fall is the busiest season in both the garden and kitchen. Our heads spin with the bounty. The kitchen crew work non-stop, cooking for today, tomorrow and the leaner months to come. Preserving can be as simple as slicing up fruits and vegetables, sealing them in a plastic bag and freezing them. Or hanging a bundle of fresh herbs in a dark basement until they're dry.

Cooking from the garden — or from the farmers' market — demands an open mind and a willingness to taste new things. This is especially true when it comes time to celebrate our Good Food for All festival each September. Hundreds of people gather in our gardens. To feed them, we need every ingredient we can get our hands on. Whatever's ready that day is what we use: butternut squash, some 30 varieties of tomatoes, a rainbow of peppers and of course the tomatillos that grow like weeds. Some recipes become instant classics.

> Our heads spin with the bounty. The kitchen crew work non-stop, cooking for today, tomorrow and the leaner months to come.

Introducing new foods — and new ways of preparing them — to our community members is one of the most rewarding things we do. Everyone feels more comfortable eating the foods they know, and this is especially true in times of adversity, when comforts are few and far between. Tomatillos are welcomed by Latino food bank users, but a lot of our members wouldn't know what to do with them if they appeared in the monthly hamper. So we organize tastings and demonstrations to show people how good new foods can taste. No matter if you're one or 101, everyone can appreciate great-tasting food. It takes time — often people won't try a new vegetable the first time around. So we set out dishes on a table in the hallway and wait. Eventually, curiosity wins out, and someone takes the first bite.

Soon people are coming back for more, and everyone's talking — about their culture's traditions, where they grew up, about the foods they ate as children. A conversation begins. –S.C.

Harvest Gazpacho

When the tomato harvest starts, the fruit comes fast and furious with over 30 varieties in our garden. At times The Stop staff bring it by the wheelbarrowful — the most gorgeous, multicoloured tomatoes you've ever laid eyes on, still warm from the sun. This gazpacho is like a burst of tomatoey sunshine, and is a terrific way to use up produce and cool down on a hot early fall day. The smoked paprika adds a distinctive flavour but can be omitted if you don't have any.

Ingredients

10 very ripe medium tomatoes, coarsely chopped

1 medium English cucumber, peeled and roughly chopped

1 red bell pepper, roughly diced

1 small red onion, roughly diced

2 cloves garlic, roughly chopped

1 8-inch piece baguette, torn into 1-inch cubes

1 cup tomato juice

2 tsp kosher salt

⅛ tsp freshly ground black pepper

2 tsp Spanish smoked paprika (optional)

¼ cup sherry or red wine vinegar

½ cup extra-virgin olive oil, plus 2 tbsp for frying bread cubes

1 clove garlic, minced

salt and pepper

Method

1. Combine tomatoes, cucumbers, bell pepper, onion, garlic and half the baguette cubes in a large bowl. Pour tomato juice over mixture and toss well, making sure to get the bread nicely soaked with the liquid. Let sit 30 minutes.

2. Preheat oven to 375°F. Arrange remaining bread cubes in a single layer on a baking sheet and toast for 10 minutes, until dry and firm. Remove from heat and allow to cool.

3. Using a blender or food processor and working in batches, purée vegetable mixture until it's very smooth and no chunks remain. Stir in salt, pepper, paprika, vinegar and olive oil. Taste and adjust seasoning as necessary. Transfer gazpacho to airtight container and refrigerate at least 4 hours or overnight to completely chill.

4. In a sauté pan, heat 2 tbsp olive oil on medium-high heat. Add garlic and stir, cooking until just lightly golden. Add toasted bread cubes and toss well to coat with garlic oil. Season with salt and pepper

5. Serve soup chilled, garnished with a few garlic croutons.

Serves 8 to 10

Butternut Squash and Apple Soup

This soup has become a favourite at our Good Food for All festival in the fall. Squash and apple are a classic combination, but you can easily use sweet potatoes, pumpkin or even carrots instead. An immersion blender is easiest, but a blender or a food processor will work if that's what you've got.

Ingredients

2 tbsp vegetable oil

1 large onion, chopped

2 cloves garlic, finely chopped

½ tsp ground nutmeg

1 large butternut squash, peeled, seeded and cut into 1-inch cubes

4 cups (or more) vegetable broth

2 Granny Smith apples, peeled, cored and diced

1 14-oz (398 mL) can coconut milk

kosher salt and freshly ground pepper

Method

1. Heat oil in large pot over medium-high heat. Add onion, garlic and nutmeg; sauté until onion begins to brown, about 5 minutes.

2. Add squash, broth, apples and coconut milk. Bring to a boil; reduce heat and simmer, uncovered, until squash and apple are tender, about 30 minutes.

3. Using an immersion blender, purée soup really well, making sure there are no lumps. Season to taste with salt and pepper. Bring soup to a simmer, thinning with more broth if desired.

Serves 4 to 6

Minestrone

When the weather starts to turn cold, there's nothing better than a warm, hearty bowl of soup. This is a lunchtime favourite at our Drop-in, served with a fresh salad and a nice piece of crusty bread for dunking. We like to top our soup with a handful of freshly grated Parmesan cheese and some hot sauce.

Ingredients

4 slices bacon, cut into ½-inch pieces

1 medium onion, diced

½ bulb fennel, greens and stalks removed, chopped into a medium dice

2 medium Yukon Gold potatoes, peeled and chopped into 1-inch pieces

3 cloves garlic, finely chopped

1 28-oz (796 mL) can whole tomatoes, lightly crushed with your hand

8 cups chicken stock or broth

1 19-oz (540 mL) can cannellini beans, drained and rinsed

2 tsp salt

½ tsp pepper

1 tsp balsamic vinegar

1 bunch Swiss chard, washed, stems removed and leaves thinly sliced

kosher salt and freshly ground pepper

1 cup small pasta (tubetti, macaroni, etc.)

1 small handful flat-leaf parsley, finely chopped

Method

1. In a soup pot over medium heat, render bacon until the meaty bits are nicely browned. Add onion, fennel and potatoes and stir to combine. Sauté for 2 minutes to sweat the onion and fennel. Add garlic and sauté another 2 minutes.

2. Add tomatoes and their juices, stock and cannellini beans; season with salt and pepper. Increase heat to high and bring to a boil. Reduce heat to a simmer and cook until potatoes are tender, about 10 minutes.

3. Add vinegar, Swiss chard and pasta and cook until pasta is al dente (tender to the touch) and chard is nicely wilted. Add parsley; taste and adjust seasoning as necessary.

Serves 6 to 8

Tip

For a vegetarian version, simply omit the bacon, use vegetable broth and vegetarian Parmesan cheese.

Curried Chicken Salad Sandwiches

These sandwiches are a joyful union of so many things: spicy, sweet, crunchy and creamy... a perfect mouthful!

Ingredients

1 skinless, boneless chicken breast

1 tsp extra-virgin olive oil

kosher salt and freshly ground pepper

1½ tbsp mayonnaise

½ tsp Dijon mustard

1 tsp curry powder

½ cup finely diced apple

¼ cup currants or raisins

½ stalk celery, finely diced

juice of ½ lemon

4 slices whole wheat or multigrain bread

¼ cup alfalfa sprouts

Method

1. Preheat oven to 425° F. Toss chicken breast with olive oil and season with salt and pepper. Arrange on a parchment-lined baking tray and roast for 20 minutes, until just cooked. Remove from heat and allow to cool.

2. In a mixing bowl, combine mayonnaise, mustard, curry powder, apple, currants, celery and lemon juice. Season with salt and pepper and stir to combine.

3. Dice chicken into 1/2-inch pieces and add to mixture. Mix well. Taste and adjust seasoning as necessary.

4. Divide chicken mixture between two slices of bread. Top each with alfalfa sprouts and a second piece of bread. Press down slightly and serve.

Makes 2

Fernando's Eggs with Tomato Chutney

On most Friday mornings, the smell of Fernando's breakfast for the Drop-in is a challenging distraction for our staff in the office. This is a really simple dish that gets gobbled up in no time.

Ingredients

2 tbsp canola oil

1 medium onion, diced

kosher salt and freshly ground pepper

1 28-oz (796 mL) can whole tomatoes, crushed with your hand, or 5 fresh plum tomatoes, diced

8 large eggs

¼ cup milk

2–3 tbsp butter

1 small handful fresh cilantro, finely chopped

Method

1. Make chutney: In a medium-sized saucepan, heat oil on medium high. Sauté onions and season lightly with salt and pepper. Add tomatoes, stir to combine and bring to a boil. Keep chutney on a low boil until about 1/3 of the liquid has evaporated and mixture has thickened.

2. Cook eggs: Heat a non-stick sauté pan on medium heat. Whisk eggs and milk together in a mixing bowl and season with salt and pepper. Melt butter in pan and swirl pan to coat bottom. Pour in egg mixture and cook for 10 seconds.

3. Draw a spatula or spoon through the egg mixture to expose the pan. Swirl the pan around to fill the space with uncooked egg. Repeat this process a few more times to build fluffiness in the eggs. Move eggs around pan until cooked and as browned as you desire. Remove from heat.

4. Add cilantro to chutney. Taste and adjust seasoning as necessary. Serve eggs with a spoonful of chutney and toast.

Serves 4

The Best Roast Beef Sandwich

Good food has the power to fuel a spirited debate, as we found out when we made these sandwiches for a community consultation on the provincial government's anti-poverty strategy. These are simple and totally satisfying.

Ingredients

2 crusty sandwich rolls, sliced in half

mayonnaise

6 slices good-quality deli roast beef

1 tomato, thinly sliced

kosher salt and freshly ground pepper

4 slices extra-old cheddar cheese

2 dill pickles, thinly sliced lengthwise

hot mustard

Method

1. Spread mayonnaise evenly on the bottom half of each roll. Layer 3 slices of roast beef on each, then 2 to 3 slices of tomato. Season with salt and pepper.

2. Lay 2 slices of cheese on top of the tomatoes, then 2 to 3 slices of pickle.

3. Spread mustard on the top half of each roll and close sandwiches. Press down slightly and slice in half.

Serves 2

Heirloom Tomato Salad

There is nothing more delicious than a summer tomato salad. Visit the market to get your hands on a variety of tomatoes for taste diversity, and some beautiful fresh basil. Our garden boasts more than 30 varieties of tomatoes, and our salads are enlivened with their juicy sweetness.

Ingredients

2 tbsp red wine vinegar

1 tsp Dijon mustard

1 tsp kosher salt

½ tsp honey

½ tsp freshly ground black pepper

½ cup extra-virgin olive oil

4 lb (2 kg) mixed heirloom tomatoes, quartered if small or cut into slices if larger

1 lb (500 g) cherry or grape tomatoes, halved

1 lb (500 g) fresh mozzarella, in tiny balls, or a large ball torn roughly into bite-size pieces

1½ cups loosely packed small basil leaves or torn large leaves

Method

1. Whisk together vinegar, mustard, salt, honey and pepper in a large bowl. Add oil in a slow stream, whisking constantly until dressing is emulsified. Add tomatoes and mozzarella and toss well. Sprinkle basil over salad and season with salt and pepper.

Serves 8 to 10

Joshna's Vegetable Chili

Use any combination of vegetables you like for this recipe. This is a great way to clean out the fridge and pantry. The bulgur is a key ingredient, adding body and texture. Buttery Cornbread (page 113) is a hearty treat alongside.

Ingredients

2 tbsp canola oil

1 medium onion, finely diced

2 stalks celery, finely diced

1 serrano or jalapeno chili, finely chopped

6 pitted black olives, finely chopped

3 cloves garlic, minced

2 tsp toasted ground cumin

1 tsp dried oregano

2 tsp chili powder

1 tsp cinnamon

1 medium bell pepper, finely diced

1 medium zucchini, finely diced

2 carrots, peeled and finely diced

1 19-oz (540 mL) can kidney beans, drained and rinsed

1 19-oz (540 mL) can chickpeas, drained and rinsed

1 19-oz (540 mL) can white beans, drained and rinsed

1 28-oz (796 mL) can whole tomatoes, puréed

1 cup store-bought salsa

1 oz (30 g) bittersweet chocolate, chopped

1 cup bulgur wheat

1 small handful fresh cilantro, chopped

1 small handful fresh parsley, chopped

kosher salt and freshly ground pepper

zest of 1 lime

1 cup sour cream

Method

1. Heat oil in a large soup pot on medium high. Add onion, celery, chili and olives and season with a pinch of salt. Stir and sauté until celery and onion are translucent but not brown. Add garlic and stir. Add cumin, oregano, chili powder and cinnamon and a good pinch of salt and pepper. Stir to combine.

2. Add chopped vegetables, all beans, puréed tomatoes, salsa and 1 cup water. Increase heat to high and bring to a boil.

3. Reduce heat and allow to simmer for about 30 minutes, or until liquid has reduced slightly. Stir often to prevent chili from sticking to the bottom of the pot. Stir in chocolate until combined.

4. At this stage, chili should be relatively thin and liquidy, as the bulgur will soak up a good bit of liquid and you don't want to dry out the dish. Add more liquid if necessary and bring back to a boil.

5. When chili is barely boiling, add bulgur and stir. Cover pot and let sit on low heat while bulgur absorbs the liquid, about 15 minutes.

6. Add fresh herbs and stir to combine. Taste and adjust seasoning.

7. In a small bowl, combine sour cream and lime zest. Set aside.

8. Serve chili with a dollop of lime sour cream and a handful of tortilla chips.   *Serves 4-6*

Cheddar Chicken Toasts

We made these in our kids' community kitchen, and they were a big hit. You can substitute almost anything for the green tomato ketchup — apricot jam or salsa would work just fine. Try sneaking some sautéed spinach under the chicken for a nice shot of greens.

Ingredients

2 boneless skinless chicken breasts

2 tsp extra-virgin olive oil

kosher salt and freshly ground pepper

4 whole wheat English muffins, sliced and toasted

⅓ cup Green Tomato Ketchup (page 110)

1 cup grated extra-old cheddar cheese

Method

1. Preheat oven to 425° F. Line a baking sheet with parchment paper and set aside. In a small bowl, combine chicken and oil; season well with salt and pepper. Toss chicken to coat well and lay out on baking sheet. Roast for 20 minutes, or until chicken is cooked through and slightly browned. Remove from heat and and set aside to cool.

2. When cool enough to handle, slice chicken into 1/4-inch slices. Spread each toasted English muffin with ketchup and set on a baking sheet lined with a fresh piece of parchment. Arrange 2 to 3 slices of chicken on each muffin half. Sprinkle cheese over chicken and toast in the oven for 15 minutes, or until cheese is nicely browned and bubbly. Let cool and serve.

Serves 4

Roasted Veggie Burritos

These are a guaranteed crowd-pleaser. Be creative and use the vegetables you have on hand. You can also add any sort of cooked meat or seafood you wish, but this veggie version is delicious and satisfying.

Ingredients

½ large eggplant, chopped into 1-inch dice

1 large sweet potato, peeled and chopped into 1-inch dice

1 large Spanish onion, peeled and cut into 1-inch-thick rings

2 handfuls button mushrooms, brushed clean

1 green zucchini, quartered lengthwise and cut into 1-inch chunks

extra-virgin olive oil

kosher salt and freshly ground pepper

4 large whole wheat tortillas

2 cups crumbled feta cheese

1 cup store-bought salsa

1 cup sour cream

zest of 1 lime

Method

1. Preheat oven to 425°F. In a large mixing bowl, toss each of the vegetables separately with olive oil (enough to coat), salt and pepper. Arrange vegetables in a single layer on parchment-lined baking sheets. You can combine the eggplant, onion, mushrooms and zucchini, but make sure the potatoes are on their own tray, as they'll take the longest to cook. Roast for 20 to 30 minutes, or until vegetables are cooked and slightly browned. Remove from heat and allow to cool slightly.

2. Combine lime zest with sour cream in a small bowl. Set aside.

3. Lay out tortillas on the counter. Combine all roasted vegetables in a bowl and toss to mix; divide among tortillas.

4. Add crumbled feta, salsa and sour cream and roll up into nice, tight bundles.

Makes 4

Vegetable Shepherd's Pie

Squash and sweet potatoes make a delicious shepherd's pie topping, and the great variety of veggies in this dish will surely keep you both interested and well nourished.

Ingredients

1 medium butternut squash, peeled, seeded and chopped into 1-inch chunks

2 medium sweet potatoes, peeled and chopped into 1-inch chunks

1 tbsp grapeseed oil

4 tbsp unsalted butter, divided

1 medium onion, finely diced

2 cloves garlic, minced

4 cups cremini mushrooms, finely chopped

2 medium green zucchini, diced

3–4 sprigs fresh thyme

1 tsp crushed dried chilies

2 cups frozen corn

kosher salt and freshly ground pepper

1 small handful flat-leaf parsley, finely chopped

¼ cup sour cream

2 tbsp finely chopped fresh chives

freshly ground nutmeg

Method

1. Combine squash and sweet potatoes in a large pot and cover with water. Season generously with salt and bring to a boil. Cook until fork-tender. Drain in colander and set aside.

2. In a high-sided sauté pan, heat oil and 2 tbsp butter on medium high. Add onion and sauté until translucent. Add garlic and cook until slightly softened but not brown. Add mushrooms, zucchini, leaves from 2 sprigs of thyme and chilies. Season with salt and pepper and stir to combine. Sauté until vegetables are softened and starting to brown.

3. Add frozen corn, remaining thyme and fresh parsley. Stir and continue to cook until corn is warmed through. Remove from heat and set aside. Preheat oven to 400° F.

4. Return drained squash and sweet potato to pot and add sour cream and remaining 2 tbsp butter. Season with salt and pepper, and mash to desired consistency. Add chives and nutmeg, and stir to combine. Taste and adjust seasoning as necessary.

5. Spread vegetable mixture evenly in the bottom of an ovenproof 9- x 13-inch dish. Spread squash mixture on top and make decorative swishes with your spatula or the tines of a fork. Bake in oven for 20 to 30 minutes, until top is toasted and filling starts to bubble. Remove from heat and allow to sit for 10 minutes.

Serves 8 to 10

Paella with Chicken

This is an easy and tasty version of the Spanish original. We used it in one of our community kitchens with a group of teenagers, and they all loved it.

Ingredients

1 chicken (about 3 lb/1.5 kg), cut into 8 pieces

6 tbsp extra-virgin olive oil

1 red bell pepper, cut into 1-inch pieces

2 lb (1 kg) tomatoes (4 medium)

4 garlic cloves, finely chopped

kosher salt

1 tsp Spanish smoked paprika

8 cups chicken stock, or reduced-sodium chicken broth

⅛ tsp crumbled saffron threads

3 cups short- or medium-grain rice like arborio or carnaroli

Method

1. Pat chicken dry and season generously with salt and pepper.

2. Heat oil in a high-sided sauté pan on high until oil is hot but not smoking. Swirl oil in pan to distribute evenly.

3. Brown chicken on all sides, turning once a crust is formed and chicken releases easily, about 8 minutes in total.

4. Move browned chicken pieces to outer edge of pan to slow down cooking while you cook the vegetables. Add bell pepper to centre of pan and sauté, stirring. Turn chicken pieces occasionally while cooking peppers, to prevent burning.

5. Add tomatoes and garlic and season with salt; cook, stirring, until mixture is thickened, about 6 minutes. Sprinkle mixture with paprika and let cook, undisturbed, for 1 minute, then stir chicken into tomato mixture.

6. Stir in stock and saffron and bring to a boil. Once boiling, sprinkle rice evenly around pan, avoiding pieces of chicken. With a wooden spoon, gently agitate mixture to make sure rice is evenly distributed and rice grains are submerged. (Do not stir again.)

7. Cook, uncovered, for 10 minutes, then reduce heat to medium and cook, covered, turning pan a quarter-turn every 5 minutes, until all liquid is absorbed and each grain of rice is distinct and just tender, 10 to 15 minutes. If all liquid has been absorbed and rice is still not tender, sprinkle tepid water, a tablespoon at a time, over rice where needed and cook for 1 or 2 minutes more.

8. Carefully remove pan from stove and let stand, covered, for 5 minutes before serving.

Serves 6

Joshna's Beef Vindaloo

We made this dish for a fundraiser with 100 pounds of donated, naturally raised beef. The magic of a vindaloo is the thick, sour, spicy gravy. Make sure you get nice hot chilies, and that you give this dish all the time it needs to marinate and simmer. Your patience will be rewarded.

Ingredients

14 cloves garlic

½ cup red wine vinegar

6 small fresh red chilies

¼ tsp cumin seeds

¾ tsp turmeric

1 tsp dry mustard

2-inch piece fresh ginger, peeled and minced

1¼ tsp kosher salt

¼ cup sugar

1 lemon

2 lb (1 kg) beef chuck, cut into 1-inch cubes

1 medium onion

ghee (clarified butter)

2 bay leaves

5 whole cloves

½ cup tomato paste

cayenne pepper, to taste

Method

1. Combine garlic, vinegar and chilies in a blender and purée to a smooth paste. In a small bowl, mix cumin, turmeric, mustard, ginger, salt and sugar together. Add this spice mixture to the blender. Peel lemon, and add only the juice and pulp to blender and mix thoroughly.

2. Marinate beef in spice mixture for 4 hours.

3. Meanwhile, finely slice onion and sauté in ghee until translucent. Add bay leaves and cloves. Increase heat to high. With a slotted spoon, lift meat out of marinade and add to frying onions to sear. When meat is seared, add marinade.

4. Cover and simmer on low for one hour. Add tomato paste and cayenne (if necessary) and simmer for another hour, until meat is nice and tender. Serve with naan.

Serves 6 to 8

Spice-Rubbed Pork Roast

Pork is quite mild and can easily hold bold flavours. The maple syrup adds a bit of sweetness to this robust rub. Of course, you can substitute pretty much any other spices for the ones listed here. Be creative — it's really hard to mess it up. The onions become soft and tender and are perfect served alongside the sliced pork. Plum Compote (page 114) is a delicious condiment for this roast.

Ingredients

2 tsp cumin seeds, toasted and ground

2 tsp dried oregano

2 tsp chili powder

1 tsp dry mustard

1 tsp kosher salt

½ tsp freshly ground black pepper

1 tbsp maple syrup

1 tbsp vegetable oil

2 cloves garlic, minced

1 large onion, peeled and sliced into 1-inch thick rings

2 lb (1 kg) boneless pork butt or loin, trimmed

Method

1. Preheat oven to 400°F. Combine cumin, oregano, chili powder, mustard, salt, pepper, maple syrup, oil and garlic in a small bowl and mix well.

2. Arrange onion slices in the centre of a roasting pan. Using your hands, rub spice mixture all over pork; put a little extra effort into it and you will be rewarded! Once the pork is well rubbed, position it on top of the onion slices and roast, basting with pan juices occasionally, for about an hour, or until pork is cooked through and a nice crust has formed around the outside (you're looking for an internal temperature of about 160°F).

3. Remove from heat and allow pork to rest for 10 minutes. Thinly slice meat against the grain and serve.

Serves 6

Cauliflower Gratin

This is an easy, reliable recipe, with a killer cheese sauce that you can use for a variety of things, including mac and cheese. You can also use different veggies for this, but the cauliflower works very well.

Ingredients

3 lb (1.5 kg) cauliflower (1 large head), cut into 1½- to 2-inch florets

½ stick (¼ cup) unsalted butter

2 tbsp all-purpose flour

1½ cups whole milk

2 cups coarsely grated sharp cheddar cheese

½ cup finely chopped scallion greens

½ tsp kosher salt

½ tsp freshly ground black pepper

20 (2-inch square) saltine crackers

Method

1. Preheat oven to 450°F. Butter a 2-quart shallow baking dish and set aside.

2. Cook cauliflower in a 5- to 6-quart pot of boiling salted water until just tender, 6 to 8 minutes. Drain cauliflower well in a colander and transfer to baking dish.

3. While cauliflower cooks, melt 2 tbsp butter in a 3- to 4-quart heavy saucepan over moderately low heat and whisk in flour. Cook this mixture whisking, for 3 minutes. Add milk in a slow stream, whisking, and bring to a boil, whisking frequently. Reduce heat and simmer sauce, whisking occasionally, for 8 minutes. Remove from heat and add cheese, scallion greens, salt and pepper, whisking until cheese is melted. Pour cheese sauce over cauliflower and stir gently to combine.

4. Coarsely crumble crackers into a bowl. Melt remaining 2 tbsp butter in a small saucepan; pour over crumbs and toss to coat.

5. Sprinkle crumb topping evenly over cauliflower. Bake gratin until topping is golden brown, about 10 minutes.

Serves 4 to 6

Salsa Verde

With its thin, paper-like husk, the tomatillo is a member of the gooseberry family. It is native to Mexico, but it also grows surprisingly well in our climate. Our garden produces incredible amounts of tomatillos, and thus our salsa verde was born! Use this as you would use any other salsa for some fresh flavour.

Ingredients

1 lb (500 g) tomatillos, husked, rinsed well and sliced in half

2 roasted poblano chilies, stem and seeds removed (see tip)

2 large green onions, roughly chopped

1 large serrano or jalapeno chili, stemmed, halved

2 large garlic cloves,

¼ cup (firmly packed) fresh cilantro leaves

1 tbsp fresh lime juice

1–2 tsp maple syrup or honey

kosher salt

Method

1. Preheat oven to 350°F. Line a baking sheet with parchment. Arrange tomatillos cut side down on baking sheet and roast in oven for about 30 minutes, or until skins start to blister and brown and tomatillos are soft. Remove from heat and allow to cool.

2. In a food processor, combine tomatillos, poblanos, green onions, chili, garlic, cilantro, lime juice and maple syrup or honey; blend until smooth and homogenous. Season well with salt and pulse to combine. Taste and adjust seasoning as necessary. Store in an airtight container in the fridge.

Makes 2 cups

Tip

You can use store-bought roasted poblanos or you can roast them yourself: place whole poblanos directly on the element of a gas stove and turn element to high (you can also do this under the broiler). Char the peppers, turning, to completely blacken the surface. Place in a bowl and cover tightly with plastic wrap; let sit for 15 minutes. Uncover bowl and rub charred skin from the flesh of the peppers. Pull out the core and seeds. Your poblanos are now ready to use. If using the broiler, remember to turn the peppers to expose all sides to the heat.

Green Tomato Ketchup

We were inspired to develop this recipe last fall when a wheelbarrowful of green tomatoes from the garden turned up. It's tangy and delicious, and can be used just like regular ketchup.

Ingredients

2 lb (1 kg) green tomatoes, washed and roughly chopped

1 yellow cooking onion, peeled and roughly chopped

¾ cup brown sugar

1 L (approximately) apple cider vinegar

kosher salt and freshly ground pepper

Method

1. In a medium-sized saucepan, combine tomatoes, onion and brown sugar. Add enough vinegar to reach just below the level of the tomatoes. Season well with salt and pepper and bring to a boil.

2. Cook at a rolling boil for 15 to 20 minutes, or until tomatoes are all cooked down and mixture has reduced a bit. Remove from heat and allow to cool.

3. Using an immersion blender, blend mixture until smooth. Taste and adjust seasoning as necessary. Store ketchup in an airtight container in the fridge for up to 2 weeks, or pour into sterilized canning jars and process for 15 minutes following the directions on the next page.

Makes 4 x 16-oz (500 mL) jars

Home Canning

Home canning is much easier than you think. It's a beautiful way to preserve the bounty of the harvest and an incredibly rewarding experience that you'll look forward to each year. Boiling water canning is the easiest method and requires a minimal amount of equipment. Pack whole fruit or vegetables into hot, sterilized jars. Cover with liquid (see tips, below) and then process in boiling water in a large stock pot, as directed.

Method

A boiling water canner is a large cooking pot with a tight-fitting lid and a wire or wooden rack that holds the jars. The pot must be deep enough to submerge the jars in briskly boiling water, with 1 to 2 inches covering the tops. The rack allows the boiling water to flow evenly around and underneath jars. It also keeps jars from bumping each other and potentially cracking or breaking.

Place jars on rack immediately after filling (up to 1/4 inch below top). Screw on sterilized lids tightly, then turn back 1/4 turn. Fill canner with water, pouring between jars, to cover the tops by 1 to 2 inches. Cover canner with lid and bring to a boil. Start timing the processing when the water comes to a rolling boil. Boil gently and steadily for the recommended time for the food being processed (follow a recipe or the chart at left). Remove jars at once and place on a rack or on towels away from heat and drafts. Let cool for 12 hours. You will hear the little pop of the lids creating a seal as they cool. This is a good thing! When jars are completely cool, press down on the top of each one to make sure all tops are sealed. You can either reprocess unsealed jars or put them in the fridge for immediate use. Store sealed jars in a cool, dry, dark place.

Processing Tips

The chart below is a list of processing times for preserving whole fruits and vegetables. For the majority of pickles, jams, relishes and butters, the recommended processing time is generally 15 to 20 minutes for pints (16 oz/500 mL) and 20 to 25 minutes for quarts (32 oz/1 L). You will need to pack fruits in a hot, thin syrup (1 cup sugar to 2 cups water, boiled for 5 minutes) and blanched vegetables in boiling water, right before processing.

Fruit/Vegetable	Pints	Quarts
crabapples, pears (peeled)	15 minutes	20 minutes
berries	10 minutes	15 minutes
rhubarb (blanched)	10 minutes	10 minutes
tomatoes (scalded & peeled)	35 minutes	45 minutes
peaches (scalded & peeled), plums, green beans	20 minutes	25 minutes
beets (cooked & skinned), carrots	15 minutes	20 minutes

Pickled Green Tomatoes

This recipe, from a long-time Stop volunteer and participant, uses underripe tomatoes. We made bottles of these pickles last year, and they were easily the favourite of all our preserves.

Ingredients

green tomatoes, sliced into ½-inch rounds

kosher salt

white vinegar

garlic, minced (1 clove per 500 mL jar)

dried oregano (½ tsp per 500 mL jar)

crushed dried red chilies (to taste)

extra-virgin olive oil

Method

DAY 1

1. Layer sliced tomatoes in a large bowl, sprinkling lots of salt over each layer. Cover bowl with a heavy plate so that the tomatoes are pressed down. Store overnight in the fridge, but be sure to put something under the bowl to catch any drips.

DAY 2

2. Drain salty water off tomatoes. Cover them with vinegar and cover with weighted plate again. Return to fridge overnight.

DAY 3

3. Drain vinegar off, squeezing out as much of the liquid as you can. Measure enough garlic, oregano and chilies for the number of sterilized jars you have and combine in a small bowl. Divide mixture evenly among jars, then cram in tomatoes. Make sure to really stuff them in and fill the space.

4. Cover tomatoes with olive oil and put the lids on the jars, tightening them and then pulling back just a bit. Following instructions on page 111, process for 15 to 20 minutes for 16-oz/500 mL jars. Turn off heat and allow to cool slightly. Remove jars from pot and place on a rack or cutting board. Allow to cool completely (you should hear the pop of the lids creating a seal during this time). When completely cool, tighten rings.

Buttery Cornbread

This is perhaps the most popular thing our kitchen produces. Served with our vegetable chili (page 98) or a soup, it makes a great meal; it also makes fantastic stuffing. The bread freezes beautifully.

Ingredients

1⅓ cups coarse stone-ground yellow cornmeal

1 cup unbleached all-purpose flour

¼ cup sugar

2 tsp baking powder

¾ tsp kosher salt

1 cup plus 2 tbsp buttermilk

9 tbsp (1 stick plus 1 tbsp) unsalted butter, melted

1 large egg plus 1 large egg yolk, beaten to blend

1 cup frozen corn kernels

1 jalapeno pepper, finely chopped

Method

1. Spray loaf pan with cooking spray and set aside.

2. Combine cornmeal, flour, sugar, baking powder and salt in a large bowl.

3. In a separate bowl, combine buttermilk, melted butter and beaten eggs and add to dry ingredients, mixing until just combined.

4. Add corn and jalapeno and stir just enough to combine. Pour batter into prepared pan and level out with spatula. Allow to sit for 30 minutes.

5. Preheat oven to 375°F. Bake bread until browned around the edges and a wooden toothpick inserted in the centre of the pan comes out clean, about 40 minutes. Remove from heat and allow to rest for 10 minutes. Turn onto a rack, slice and serve.

Makes 1 loaf

Plum Compote

This is a perfect condiment for our spice-rubbed pork (page 106). Fresh thyme and balsamic vinegar give the sweet plums a bold, savoury flavour.

Ingredients

1 lb (500g) small red plums (about 8)

½ tsp salt

½ tsp freshly ground pepper

1 tbsp chopped fresh thyme leaves

2 tbsp extra-virgin olive oil

½ cup apple juice

2 tbsp balsamic vinegar

Method

1. Slice plums in half and remove pits. Combine plum halves in a mixing bowl with salt, pepper and thyme. Toss gently to coat.

2. Heat olive oil in a large skillet over medium heat. Place plum halves cut-side down in the skillet; cook, shaking skillet often, until plums release their juices but still hold together, 5 to 6 minutes. Add apple juice and vinegar; cook until the juice thickens slightly, about 2 minutes more.

Serves 8

Social Justice

In one of the hallways at The Stop, a child's drawing of a pink bunny with orange carrots has been taped to the wall. The caption scrawled on the picture reads: "I will use my carrots to rule the world!"

A bunch of carrots may not sound revolutionary (even if it is sustainably grown in our community gardens and carefully cooked in our kitchens). But imagine what could happen if everyone across Canada — or North America, even the world — insisted that access to nutritious, sustainably produced foods is a universal human right.

At The Stop, we've been imagining exactly that, working for more than 10 years to marry our front-line food programs with advocacy for social justice. Through programs that aim to both educate and empower, The Stop provides a platform for community members to take charge of their lives and advocate for social and political change. Participants learn about the political process and how to access vital community services, as well as how to make sure their stories are heard by those in positions of power. We ensure that people have the tools to challenge a system that forces them to make impossible choices between paying the rent or putting food on the table.

Food can be a great connector — growing it, eating it, sharing it — and we think it also has the potential to work as a transformative political tool. A bunch of carrots — and the principles that brought them to our kitchen — can organize a community. They can tell a story more effectively than a cabinet minister's dossier. In the right hands, we're certain that food does have the power to change the world. –*S.C.*

Sweet Potato Tarts

We first made these tarts for an African Heritage Expo, but they have become a crowd favourite and we now make them for many of our special events. The recipe is easy and you can fancy it up with a little dollop of sweetened lime cream. The tart mixture freezes really well.

Ingredients

2 large red-skinned sweet potatoes (1¼ – 1½ lb/625 – 750 g)

1 cup packed golden brown sugar

¾ cup whipping cream

¾ cup orange juice

3 large eggs

1 tsp vanilla extract

½ tsp salt

¼ tsp ground nutmeg

1 tsp cinnamon

24 frozen mini-tart shells

Method

1. Preheat oven to 400°F. Pierce potatoes with a fork, then roast until a knife slides through the centre easily. Remove from heat and allow to cool.

2. When cool enough to handle, scrape potato flesh into a bowl; mash until smooth. Measure out 1 1/2 cups potato purée.

3. Position rack in bottom third of oven. Place purée in a large bowl. Whisk in brown sugar, cream, juice, eggs, vanilla, salt, nutmeg and cinnamon; pour mixture into a pitcher. Arrange tart shells on a baking sheet, and carefully pour filling into tart shells.

4. Bake tarts until filling is puffed around edges and set in centre, about 25 minutes. Transfer to a rack to cool.

Makes 24 tarts

Pumpkin Chocolate Chip Squares

We make these often with kids and youth groups, and they are always a hit. You certainly can roast your own pumpkin and scoop out the flesh, but this is one of those times when a canned product is just fine.

Ingredients

2 cups spelt flour

1 tsp cinnamon

½ tsp nutmeg

½ tsp ground cloves

½ tsp ground ginger

1 tsp baking soda

¾ tsp salt

1 cup (2 sticks) unsalted butter, at room temperature

1¼ cups sugar

1 large egg

2 tsp vanilla extract

1 cup canned pumpkin purée

1 pkg (12 oz/340 g) semi-sweet chocolate chips

Method

1. Preheat oven to 350°F. Butter and flour a 9- x 13-inch baking pan and set aside. In a medium-sized bowl, whisk together flour, spices, baking soda and salt; set aside.

2. With an electric mixer, cream butter and sugar on medium-high speed until smooth; beat in egg and vanilla until combined. Beat in pumpkin purée (mixture may appear curdled... it's okay!) Reduce speed to low and mix in dry ingredients until just combined. Fold in chocolate chips.

3. Spread batter evenly in prepared pan. Bake until edges begin to pull away from sides of pan and a wooden toothpick inserted in centre comes out with just a few moist crumbs attached, 35 to 40 minutes. Cool completely in pan.

4. Cut into squares and serve.

Makes one 9- x 13-inch pan

Spiced Applesauce

This is a perfect way to enjoy Ontario apples. You can store the applesauce in an airtight container in the fridge for up to 2 weeks, you can freeze it, or you can process it in sterilized canning jars for 15 minutes in a boiling water bath (page 111).

Ingredients

3 lb (1.5 kg) apples, peeled, cored, cut into ¾-inch pieces

1 cup water

⅓ cup packed brown sugar

3–4 cardamom pods

2½ tbsp fresh lemon juice

1 tsp cinnamon

Method

1. Combine apples, water, brown sugar and cardamom pods in a heavy, medium-sized saucepan. Bring to a boil, stirring occasionally. Reduce heat, cover and simmer until apples are very tender, about 25 minutes. Uncover and simmer until almost all liquid has evaporated, about 6 minutes. Remove from heat. Stir in lemon juice and cinnamon. Cool 30 minutes.

2. Using a potato masher, mash apple mixture until coarse and chunky. Fish out cardamom pods. Serve at room temperature or refrigerate until cold.

Makes about 3 cups

buttercup squash
brussels sprouts
cranberries garlic
kohlrabi turnips
carrots crabapples
spaghetti squash
jerusalem artichoke
pears leeks **winter**
parsnips potatoes
rutabaga cabbage
sweet potatoes

Winter Celebration

After the frenetic pace of the fall harvest, we're all ready for the winter slowdown. Finally, it's time to come indoors, turn on the ovens and catch our breath. If slow cooking has a season, this is it: there's nothing like a pot of Easy Chicken Curry (page 132) bubbling merrily on the stove, or the smell of a Hearty Beef Stew (page 137) as it cooks in the oven. When the temperature drops, the cozy comforts of soups and roasts are a welcome change from salad days.

Winter is a time for potluck dinners and large meals served family-style. All the stews and casseroles and cakes here are meant to be shared — with family, friends or the community. And so many cold-weather foods taste even better as leftovers. Soups and stews can just be reheated; a roast chicken or leftover jerk chicken (page 134) can be transformed into chilaquiles (page 130), a Mexican breakfast casserole.

At The Stop, winter is also a time for celebrations, starting with the winter solstice. Because so many people at our centre come from different places in the world, we celebrate practically every holiday on the planet. Pear Spice Cake (page 148), is an exceptional celebration cake, as we discovered when we baked it for our Healthy Beginnings program. But the best recipes often come from our participants themselves, like the hearty vegetable stew (page 140) that one native of Colombia taught us to make.

Holiday time epitomizes the generosity of spirit at The Stop. Visit our kitchen, and chances are you won't leave empty-handed. Try Joshna's yummy granola (page 150) in your own kitchen. Tied up with ribbon or string, it makes a thoughtful hostess gift.

Winter is a time for potluck dinners and large meals served family-style.

Of course, the cold season can be bittersweet for gardeners. Though the frost sweetens the carrots, squash and kale, it's also time to plant a cover crop of rye and vetch, tidy up for the big sleep and begin the long wait for springtime.

In winter, we buy more of our produce from farmers and markets to ensure healthy food for our programs. Though our funds are always limited, we try to be conscientious in our purchasing. It's always a trade-off: we want to buy the most food we can for the least money, while still sourcing as much as possible from local farmers. It's our greatest challenge, and it's an important part of who we are. Because good food should be for everyone. –*S.C.*

Red Lentil and Carrot Soup

This is an earthy soup, perfect for warming up on a cool evening. There's a bit of spice for a nice hit at the back of your throat, and the crumbled feta is surprisingly tasty.

Ingredients

2 tbsp vegetable oil

1 cup chopped onion

3 garlic cloves, minced

1 tsp ground coriander

1 tsp ground cumin

¼ tsp turmeric

cayenne to taste

¾ lb (375 g) red lentils, picked over (about 1⅔ cup)

7 cups vegetable/chicken stock or water

5 carrots, halved lengthwise and sliced thinly crosswise

1 cup finely chopped red bell pepper

1 handful fresh cilantro, finely chopped

¼ cup chopped scallion, greens only

kosher salt and freshly ground pepper

¼ cup crumbled feta

fresh cilantro sprigs

Method

1. In a medium-sized saucepan, heat oil on medium-high heat. Sauté onion until translucent, then add garlic and cook for 1 minute more. Add coriander, cumin, turmeric and cayenne and stir to combine. Add lentils and stock or water and bring to a boil. Simmer gently, partially covered, for 15 minutes, occasionally skimming froth off the top if necessary, until lentils are just less than tender.

2. Stir in carrots and red pepper and simmer another 10 minutes, until carrots are tender.

3. Stir in cilantro, scallion greens, cayenne, and salt and pepper to taste.

4. Serve soup garnished with crumbled feta and cilantro sprigs.

Serves 4

Bold Green Salad with Flaxseed Vinaigrette

Be creative with this salad: try different combinations of greens and flavours in the vinaigrette. The flaxseed oil doesn't overpower the taste of the dressing at all — and you're getting a great dose of essential fatty acids. You can store the vinaigrette in the fridge in an airtight container for up to two weeks.

Ingredients

3 medium beets

1 tbsp minced shallot

1 tsp Dijon mustard

¼ cup apple cider vinegar

1 clove garlic, minced

1 tbsp maple syrup

1 tsp kosher salt

½ tsp freshly ground pepper

2 tbsp flaxseed oil

½ cup grapeseed or extra-virgin olive oil

4 large handfuls mixed salad greens (arugula, spinach, endive, dandelion, lettuce, etc.)

1 handful sprouts (pea, onion, broccoli)

6 oz (170 g) chèvre (goat cheese)

1 small handful walnut halves, toasted and roughly chopped

Method

1. Preheat oven to 350°F. Place unpeeled beets in an oven-proof casserole dish; pour 2 cm of water into the bottom. Cover tightly with foil and roast for about 2 hours, or until a knife slides through beets easily. Remove from heat and allow to cool. Peel beets and cut into wedges. Set aside.

2. Make vinaigrette: place shallot, mustard, vinegar, garlic and maple syrup in a medium bowl and whisk together. Season with salt and pepper.

3. While whisking, drizzle in flaxseed oil, then grapeseed or olive oil to make a smooth emulsion. Taste and adjust seasoning as necessary.

4. In a large salad bowl, combine greens, sprouts and half the vinaigrette and toss gently to coat. Divide salad among the plates. Add 2 or 3 beet wedges to each salad, then crumble chèvre over beets. Finish with a sprinkle of walnuts and a little drizzle of vinaigrette on top.

Serves 4 to 6

Carrot Salad

We once used Pfenning's beautiful organic carrots (from a southern Ontario farm) as our food of the month and did demos of this recipe in the food bank to show community members what they could do with their carrots. This pretty salad is shown with our Roast Sausages with Kale on page 139.

Ingredients

3 large carrots, peeled and grated

2 scallions, very finely chopped

1 small handful flat-leaf parsley, very finely chopped

1 handful raisins

3–4 tbsp vegetable oil

2 tbsp cider vinegar

½ tsp ground cumin

kosher salt and freshly ground pepper

Method

1. In a mixing bowl, combine all ingredients and toss well to mix. Taste and adjust seasoning as necessary. Set aside for about 15 minutes for flavours to blend.

Serves 4 to 6

Easy Coleslaw

Everyone likes a good tangy, crunchy coleslaw. Letting this sit for a little while before serving really gives the flavours a chance to make friends. This is great as a side dish for Joshna's Jerk Chicken (page 134) or on a sandwich.

Ingredients

¼ cup extra-virgin olive oil

¼ cup mayonnaise

½ cup white vinegar

1 tsp Dijon mustard

2 tsp honey

1 tsp kosher salt

½ tsp freshly ground pepper

3 cups green cabbage, shredded (about ½ cabbage)

2 cups peeled and shredded carrots

½ small white onion, shredded

Method

1. Combine olive oil, mayonnaise, vinegar, mustard, honey, salt and pepper in a small bowl and whisk together.

2. In a large bowl, toss together cabbage, carrots and onion. Pour vinaigrette over cabbage mixture and toss well with your hands to coat the slaw completely with the vinaigrette. Allow to sit for 15 minutes before serving.

Serves 6

Classic Balsamic Vinaigrette

This is a perfect vinaigrette for winter salads featuring bitter greens, mushrooms and dried fruit. But to be honest, it's good on almost anything, including grain salads and baked potatoes.

Ingredients

¼ cup balsamic vinegar

1 clove garlic, minced

½ tsp dried basil

1 tsp Dijon mustard

2 tsp maple syrup

kosher salt and freshly ground pepper

½ cup extra-virgin olive oil

Method

1. In a small bowl, whisk together vinegar, garlic, basil, mustard, maple syrup, salt and pepper.

2. Place a kitchen towel under your bowl to steady it and while whisking, drizzle in olive oil in a thin stream. Whisk until oil is completely incorporated and mixture is smooth and emulsified. Taste and adjust seasoning as necessary. Store in the fridge in an airtight container.

Makes about 1 cup

Chilaquiles

Chilaquiles are a Mexican breakfast casserole, usually made from the previous night's leftovers. The ingredients may seem really simple, but in this dish the whole is much greater than the sum of the parts. You can easily substitute any leftovers you have for the cooked chicken; we've used roasted sweet potatoes, peppers and even mushrooms with great success. A nice fiery salsa makes this dish really pop.

Ingredients

1 cup sour cream

3 tbsp milk

zest of 1 lime

1¾ cups salsa verde (page 109)

1¾ cups low-sodium chicken broth

3 cups cooked chicken, shredded

6 cups tortilla chips, or 6 small day-old corn tortillas, torn into bite-size pieces and toasted until crisp

kosher salt and freshly ground pepper

½ cup crumbled feta (2 oz/60 g)

½ cup finely chopped scallion greens

¼ cup chopped fresh cilantro

Method

1. Stir just enough milk into sour cream to give it a thick but pourable consistency. Add lime zest, stir and set aside.

2. In a high-sided sauté pan, bring salsa and broth to a boil. Add chicken, season well with salt and pepper, and cook, stirring, until chicken is heated through, 1 to 2 minutes.

3. Stir in tortilla chips and cook until chips are softened (but not mushy), about 1 minute.

4. Transfer chilaquiles to a large platter and sprinkle with feta, scallion greens and cilantro. Serve immediately with lime sour cream on the side.

Serves 6

Jan 20/10
v. good & easy - needs rice with it

Easy Chicken Curry

Chicken curry is still one of my all-time favourite foods. This is a slightly quicker version of the original, and it's a great way to get your feet wet with Indian cooking. Feel free to adjust masala quantities to your taste.

Ingredients

3 tbsp vegetable oil or ghee

2 tsp cumin seeds

1 green chili, sliced in half lengthwise

4–5 fresh (or dried) curry leaves

2 yellow cooking onions, finely chopped

2 tbsp minced garlic

1 tsp minced gingerroot

1½ tsp cayenne

2 tsp ground coriander

1 tbsp ground cumin

1 tsp turmeric

kosher salt and freshly ground pepper to taste

2 lb (1 kg) boneless skinless chicken, such as breasts and thighs, chopped into 1-inch pieces

1½ cups puréed tomatoes

1 tbsp garam masala

finely chopped fresh cilantro and lime wedges to garnish

Method

1. In a heavy-bottomed saucepan, heat the oil or ghee on high. Add cumin seeds, chili and curry leaves and stand back! Once the spluttering has subsided, reduce heat to medium-high, add the onions and fry for about 4 minutes, until they turn a rich golden brown.

2. Add the garlic and ginger and sauté until soft and starting to brown. Mix in the cayenne, ground coriander, cumin, turmeric, salt and pepper. Sauté briefly to cook and combine.

3. Increase the heat to high and add the chicken pieces. Toss to coat with onions and spices, and fry for about 5 minutes or until the chicken is well coated in the spice mixture and lightly browned.

4. Add the tomatoes and mix well. Bring to a boil. Reduce heat to low, cover and simmer for about 15 minutes or until chicken is well cooked. Sprinkle in the garam masala, cover again, and continue to simmer for about 10 to 15 minutes to allow the aromas to blend well in the curry. The longer this simmers on low, the better the flavour will be. Taste and adjust salt and chili as necessary. (Fish out the 2 halves of chili, if desired.) Serve hot, garnished with chopped cilantro and lime wedges.

Serves 4 to 6

Here's a list of the most common spices and aromatics in Indian cooking. These flavours anchor so many Indian dishes; they are useful pantry items to have on hand.

Item	What It Is	Where to Find It
ghee	toasted, clarified butter	Indian grocery stores, some large grocery stores, or make your own (see tip)
cumin	spice, used whole or toasted and ground; warm spicy flavour	spice shops, Indian grocery stores, some large grocery stores
coriander	spice, used whole or toasted and ground; bright flavour	spice shops, Indian grocery stores, some large grocery stores
cilantro	fresh herb, stems and leaves used	most grocery stores and produce markets, Asian markets
turmeric	spice, ground from a dried root; mild earthy flavour	spice shops, Indian grocery stores, some large grocery stores
curry leaves	fresh or dried leaves	Indian grocery stores, or you can grow your own indoors
garam masala	spice mixture of sweet, earthy spices, used to finish curries	Indian grocery stores, spice shops, or you can make your own
green chili	long, thin green chili with clean, bright heat	Indian grocery stores

Tip

To make your own ghee, simply melt unsalted butter gently in a small, heavy-bottomed pan. Skim off and discard the white foam on top, and pour off the clear melted butter (ghee), leaving behind the milky residue at the bottom (the milk solids). Ghee can be refrigerated for several weeks in an airtight container.

Joshna's Jerk Chicken

This is a huge crowd-pleaser, and much easier to make than you think. Giving the chicken the chance to marinate overnight is really the key to success, as the meat becomes saturated with all that great flavour. Another secret is cooking the chicken long and low... remember, nothing is rushed in the islands. Serve with Classic Rice and Peas (page 146) and Easy Coleslaw (page 128).

Ingredients

⅓ cup vegetable oil

¼ cup white vinegar

2 tbsp fresh lime juice

2 tbsp ground allspice

2 tsp kosher salt

2 tsp freshly ground pepper

1 tbsp finely chopped gingerroot

1 tsp brown sugar

½ tsp ground cinnamon

3 large sprigs fresh thyme

5 scallions, finely chopped

2 cloves garlic, minced

Scotch bonnet pepper sauce, to taste

1 4-lb (2-kg) chicken, cut into 8 pieces, or 12 drumsticks

Method

1. In a small bowl, combine oil, vinegar, lime juice, allspice, salt, pepper, ginger, sugar, cinnamon and thyme. Add the scallions, garlic and pepper sauce to the oil mixture and stir well.

2. In a large mixing bowl, place the chicken pieces and pour spice mixture over them. Wearing gloves, massage the spice mixture into the chicken with your hands. Marinate, covered and refrigerated, for at least 5 hours or overnight.

3. Preheat the oven to 350°F. Line a baking sheet with parchment paper.

4. Spread marinated chicken on the baking sheet, leaving a bit of room between pieces. Pour the remaining marinade over chicken and roast for 35 to 40 minutes or until the chicken is cooked through and juices run clear. There should be a nicely browned crust, but the chicken should still be plump and juicy. Discard the thyme sprigs before serving.

Serves 5 to 6

Tip

For a vegetarian version we have successfully substituted the same weight of firm tofu for the chicken. Tofu is the ultimate blank slate for flavour, and a perfect vehicle for this bold marinade. I still recommend marinating the tofu overnight, but I also brush some of the marinade on it before roasting so it develops a nice sticky, spicy crust.

Health

"He who takes medicine and neglects diet wastes the skill of the physician," goes an old Chinese proverb. Long before the advent of nutritionists and "functional" foods, the ancients considered good food essential to good health, the first line of defence against myriad illnesses and diseases. And as we delve deeper and deeper into this field of research, such beliefs have been vindicated. Today we can cite scientific studies that link diet to various illnesses, from Type 2 diabetes to cardiovascular disease and some forms of cancer.

It seems like a no-brainer: eat well and be healthy. The trouble is good food doesn't come cheap. Just look at the well-heeled shoppers filling their carts with organic quinoa and $10-a-pound grapes at Whole Foods. For people on a tight budget, it's tempting to fill that shopping cart with inexpensive, calorie-dense processed foods instead of those packed with nutrients. Canada's Food Guide is all very well for the middle class, but for food bank users on welfare, that pyramid can look more like economic elitism.

That's why, whenever possible, we supplement The Stop's monthly food hampers with produce bought from local farmers or grown in our own gardens — fresh, organic ingredients that would otherwise be unaffordable. But providing a community with access to whole foods is only the first step. Cooking with raw ingredients requires kitchen skills — skills that have become increasingly rare in an age of Twinkies and Pop-Tarts, when so much of the food available to consumers is cheap, fast and convenient. After all, it's much easier to open a bag of chips than to figure out what to do with a sack of potatoes.

Tackling this knowledge gap head-on, we offer a number of programs to engage our community, from cooking classes for recent immigrants to Healthy Beginnings, which encourages new mothers to buy and prepare healthy, inexpensive food for themselves and their babies. The latest proof that prevention is the best cure? Ninety-eight per cent of babies born to our mothers achieve a healthy birth weight. –S.C.

Jan. 2010   Excellent stew.

Hearty Beef Stew

There is nothing better than a stew cooked long and low on a cold day. Substitute potatoes or parsnips for the carrots, or use a mixture if you like. Serve with a hunk of good crusty bread.

Ingredients

3 lb (1.5 kg) stewing beef, cut into 1½-inch cubes

1½ tsp kosher salt

1 tsp freshly ground pepper

2–3 tsp vegetable oil

2 medium-large onions, chopped

3 garlic cloves, minced

3 tbsp all-purpose flour

1 cup red wine

2 cups homemade beef broth or low-sodium store-bought broth

2 bay leaves

3 sprigs fresh thyme, or 1 tsp dried

4 large carrots, peeled and sliced into ¼-inch-thick half-moons

1 cup frozen peas, thawed

1 small handful fresh parsley, minced

Method

1. Preheat oven to 300°F. Place meat in a large bowl. Sprinkle with salt and pepper; toss to coat.

2. Heat 2 tablespoons oil over medium-high heat in a high-sided sauté pan; add meat to pan in two batches. Brown meat on all sides, about 5 minutes per batch, adding an additional 1 tablespoon oil if necessary. Transfer meat to a platter.

3. Add onions to pan; sauté until almost softened, 4 to 5 minutes. Reduce heat to medium and add garlic; continue to sauté for about 30 seconds longer. Stir in flour and cook until lightly coloured, 1 to 2 minutes. Stir in wine, scraping up any browned bits that have stuck to the pan. Add beef broth, bay leaves and thyme; bring to simmer. Add browned meat and carrots and return to a simmer. Cover and place in oven, and simmer until meat is just tender, 2 1/2 to 3 hours.

4. Add uncooked peas to fully cooked stew; cover and let stand to blend flavours, about 5 minutes. Stir in parsley, adjust seasoning and serve.

Serves 6 to 8

add a tsp of Balsamic vinegar

Roast Sausages with Kale

The bitterness of the greens with the richness of the sausage make for a great mouthful. Serve this with a grain salad, Saffron Couscous with Herbs (page 147), Carrot Salad (page 127) or even some roasted potatoes for a lovely lunch.

Ingredients

4 fresh sausages (Italian, kielbasa, chorizo, etc.)

2–3 tbsp vegetable oil

1 red onion, peeled and sliced

2 cloves garlic, sliced

1 bunch kale, washed, stems removed and leaves torn into large pieces

kosher salt and freshly ground pepper

juice of 1 lemon

Method

1. Preheat oven to 425° F. Line a baking sheet with parchment and arrange sausages with a bit of room between them. Roast for 15 to 20 minutes, or until cooked through and nicely browned.

2. Meanwhile, heat vegetable oil on high in a large sauté pan. Add onions, season lightly with salt and stir. When onions start becoming translucent, add garlic and stir. When onions are starting to brown, add kale, season with salt and pepper and cover. Reduce heat to medium high and allow to cook for 5 to 7 minutes, or until kale is wilted and tender.

3. Season with lemon juice and stir to combine. Taste and adjust seasoning as necessary. Serve with roasted sausages.

Serves 4

Vegetable Ajiaco

This delicious recipe for Columbian vegetable stew came from one of the participants in our Healthy Beginnings program. The soup is quite hearty and plays beautifully with fresh and cooked elements.

Ingredients

3 tbsp olive oil

1 large white onion, finely chopped

2 tsp dried oregano, crumbled

1 tsp kosher salt

1 tsp freshly ground pepper

1½ lb (750 g) russet (baking) potatoes

4 medium carrots, chopped into ½-inch slices

2 cups fresh button mushrooms, chopped in half

1 medium zucchini, finely diced

6 cups vegetable broth

2 lb (1 kg) Yukon Gold potatoes, peeled, cut into ½-inch cubes, and covered with water in a bowl

3 ears corn, husks removed, cut crosswise into 1-inch pieces

ACCOMPANIMENTS:
½ cup chopped fresh cilantro

1 cup 35% cream (optional)

3 ripe avocados, quartered, pitted, peeled, and cut into ½-inch cubes

Method

1. Heat olive oil in a wide, heavy 7- to 8-quart pot over moderately high heat. Add onion to pot along with oregano and salt and pepper, and sauté, stirring, until light golden, about 5 minutes. Peel and coarsely grate russet potatoes and add to pot along with carrots, mushrooms, zucchini and broth.

2. Simmer, covered, stirring occasionally, until vegetables are cooked through, about 25 minutes. Drain cubed yellow potatoes and add to pot. Simmer, covered, stirring occasionally, until cubed potatoes are almost tender, about 10 minutes. Add corn and simmer, covered, until tender, 5 to 10 minutes more.

3. Serve stew. At the table, pass cilantro, avocado and cream to stir into stew.

Serves 6

Vegetable Rundown

"Rundown" is a classic stew served throughout the Caribbean, usually made with chicken, fish and vegetables. The name refers to the length of time this dish is cooked: it's a long and low reduction to really develop the flavour. Serve with rice or crusty bread for a hearty meal.

Ingredients

1 medium eggplant (1–1¼ lb/ 500–625 g)), unpeeled, cut into 1-inch pieces

1 tsp kosher salt

1 tbsp vegetable oil

2 cups chopped onions

¾ cup chopped green onions, divided

3 large fresh thyme sprigs

2 garlic cloves, chopped

1 tsp ground allspice

½ Scotch bonnet pepper, seeded and minced (½ tsp)

1 14-oz (398 mL) can unsweetened coconut milk

1 lb (500 g) sweet potatoes, peeled, cut into ¾-inch pieces

1 cup (or more) water

4 cups coarsely chopped green cabbage (about ¼ large head)

2 cups fresh corn kernels (from 2 ears of corn) or frozen

kosher salt and freshly ground pepper

Method

1. Place eggplant in a colander set over a bowl. Sprinkle with salt; let stand 20 minutes. Rinse and drain.

2. Heat oil in large, heavy pot over medium-high heat. Add onions, 1/2 cup green onions, thyme, garlic, allspice and minced pepper; sauté until onions are tender, about 8 minutes. Add coconut milk and simmer 3 minutes. Add sweet potato and 1 cup water and return to a simmer. Sprinkle with salt and pepper. Cover and simmer until vegetables are almost tender, stirring occasionally, about 10 minutes.

3. Add eggplant, cabbage and corn to vegetable mixture. If necessary, add enough water to partially cover vegetables. Cover and simmer until all vegetables are tender and mixture is thick and creamy, about 15 minutes longer; during this time, stir often and add more water by 1/4 cupfuls if liquid is too thick. Season to taste with salt and pepper. Transfer stew to bowl; sprinkle with remaining 1/4 cup green onions and serve.

Serves 4 to 6

Zucchini Bake

This recipe is a favourite of our garden staff. You can easily substitute potatoes, sweet potatoes, carrots or beets for the zucchini, or even mix a couple together. Serve with applesauce or a salsa.

Ingredients

2 tsp extra-virgin olive oil

1 large or 2 small zucchini

3 cups grated cheese, such as mozzarella or cheddar

2 tsp baking powder

1 tsp kosher salt

½ tsp freshly ground pepper

3 tbsp flour

½ cup milk

4 eggs

Method

1. Preheat oven to 375° F. Grease a 9-inch square pan with olive oil. Grate zucchini and spread it in an even layer in the pan. Place grated cheese on top of zucchini.

2. In a medium-sized bowl, mix together the baking powder, salt, pepper and flour, then whisk in the milk and eggs. Pour evenly over zucchini and cheese.

3. Bake for about 35 minutes, or until nicely browned and cooked through. Remove from heat and allow to cool slightly. Cut into squares and serve.

Serves 4

Mari/10 good!

Tofu Baked Bean Casserole

This dish was created by accident one day when we received a big donation of baked beans, and the fridge was full of produce. You can use virtually any vegetables you like in place of the eggplant, zucchini and peppers, but just remember to group them in terms of how long they take to cook. Don't combine root veggies, for instance, with softer zucchini and peppers. Frying the tofu beforehand helps it keep its shape, and infuses it with garlicky goodness. Serve with rice or nice hunks of bread.

Ingredients

½ large eggplant,
cut into 1-inch cubes

2 medium zucchini,
cut into 1-inch cubes

1 red bell pepper,
cut into 1-inch pieces

¼ vegetable oil, plus enough
to coat vegetables

kosher salt and freshly
ground pepper

3 cloves garlic, divided

1 lb (500 g) firm tofu, drained
and cut into 1-inch cubes

1 onion, peeled and coarsely
chopped

2 14-oz (398 mL) cans
baked beans

1 small handful parsley,
finely chopped

2 cups grated shredded cheese
such as mozzarella, cheddar,
Parmesan, etc.

Method

1. Preheat oven to 425° F. Line 2 baking sheets with parchment and set aside. In a mixing bowl, toss eggplant, zucchini and bell pepper with enough vegetable oil to coat and season well with salt and pepper. Spread out on baking sheets, creating an even single layer on each. Roast vegetables for about 20 minutes, or until they're nicely browned but bell pepper is still a bit crisp. Remove from heat and reduce oven temperature to 350° F. Place roasted veggies in a large mixing bowl and set aside.

2. In a sauté pan, heat 1/4 cup vegetable oil on medium-high heat. Slice 1 clove of garlic in thirds and fry in oil 1 minute, being careful not to brown. Add tofu and fry until golden brown, turning if necessary. Remove tofu from oil and drain on a paper-towel-lined plate. Using a slotted spoon, fish out the garlic and discard. Return pan to heat. Sauté onion until translucent and season with salt and pepper. Finely chop remaining garlic cloves and add to pan; sauté for 1 minute more, then add mixture to the bowl of roasted veggies. Add the baked beans, tofu and parsley to mixture and stir well to combine. Spread mixture into a 9- x 13-inch baking pan or casserole dish and sprinkle shredded cheese on top.

3. Bake for 10 to 15 minutes until cheese is browned and mixture starts to bubble at the sides of the pan.

Serves 4 to 6

Classic Rice and Peas

This rice dish has a lovely creaminess. The secret? Using coconut milk and the water from the canned peas as the cooking liquid. It is so flavourful and complex you don't need anything on top. This tasty side dish is shown with Joshna's Jerk Chicken on page 135.

Ingredients

**1 19-oz (540 mL) can
pigeon peas, turtle beans
or kidney beans**

2 cups coconut milk

2 scallions, finely chopped

1 whole Scotch bonnet pepper

½ tsp dried thyme

½ tsp kosher salt

½ tsp freshly ground pepper

2 cups long grain white rice

1 tbsp butter

Method

1. In a large measuring cup, combine the liquid from the canned peas with the coconut milk. Add more water if necessary to make 3 1/2 cups of liquid. Pour the liquid into a large saucepan and add the peas, scallions, hot pepper, thyme, salt and black pepper. Stir, bring to a boil and cook for 3 minutes.

2. Add the rice and butter; stir the pot once, but be careful not to burst the pepper or this will become way too hot! Reduce heat to low, cover, and simmer for about 25 minutes or until the water has been completely absorbed and the rice is cooked. Don't be tempted to lift the lid and check on it for at least 20 minutes — you'll lose all that good steam. If the rice is still not tender after the water is absorbed, add 2 to 4 tbsp of water, cover and simmer for another 5 to 10 minutes. Fluff lightly with a fork and serve.

Serves 4 to 6

Saffron Couscous with Herbs

This is a perfectly easy side dish that's full of flavour. Serve with a piece of fish, chicken or beef, or as a base for a stew or grilled vegetables. This dish is pictured alongside Roast Sausages with Kale on page 139.

Delicious

Ingredients

2 tbsp sesame seeds

2 tbsp pine nuts

2 cups chicken or vegetable stock

1 pinch saffron

2 cups couscous (whole wheat or regular)

1 tbsp butter

½ small onion, finely diced

3–4 tbsp extra-virgin olive oil

2–3 tbsp lemon juice

red pepper flakes, to taste

¼ cup sultana raisins

½ cup each finely chopped fresh mint, cilantro and parsley

kosher salt and freshly ground pepper

Method

1. Preheat oven to 400° F. Spread sesame seeds and pine nuts on a cookie sheet and bake until golden, about 5 minutes. Be careful, because these will burn easily. Transfer to a bowl and set aside.

2. In a large saucepan, place stock with saffron and 1/4 tsp salt and bring to a boil. Remove from heat and add couscous. Stir, cover with plastic wrap and let stand for 15 minutes.

3. Heat butter in a small sauté pan on medium-high heat. Sauté chopped onion and season with a bit of salt; cook until onion is translucent and slightly browned. Set aside.

4. Fluff couscous with a fork and toss with olive oil, lemon juice, red pepper flakes, salt and pepper. Add sesame seeds, pine nuts, raisins, sautéed onion and fresh herbs. Toss gently, taste and adjust seasoning as necessary.

Serves 4 8

needs lots of lemon juice + herbs.

Pear Spice Cake

We made this cake for a Healthy Beginnings holiday celebration meal and served a dollop of cinnamon whipped cream on each piece. It's a delicious cake, and wholesome, too.

Ingredients

cooking spray

3 cups spelt flour, plus more for pan

1 tbsp ground cinnamon

1 tsp baking soda

1 tsp salt

1⅓ cups vegetable oil

2 cups packed brown sugar

3 large eggs

3–4 Bartlett pears, peeled, cored and cut into ½-inch pieces (3 cups)

1 cup chopped assorted nuts, such as pecans and walnuts (optional)

1 tsp vanilla extract

Method

1. Preheat oven to 350° F. Spray a 9-inch square baking pan with cooking spray and dust lightly with flour; set aside.

2. Working over a large sheet of parchment paper, sift together flour, cinnamon, baking soda and salt; gather sifted ingredients into centre of sheet; set aside.

3. In a large mixing bowl, whisk together vegetable oil, brown sugar and eggs until well combined and a bit frothy.

4. Fold reserved parchment in half lengthwise and gradually shake dry ingredients into liquid mixture; mix with a spatula until just incorporated.

5. Add pears and, if desired, nuts, to batter; mix to combine. Add vanilla, mixing until incorporated.

6. Pour batter into prepared pan and bake until a wooden toothpick inserted in the centre comes out clean, 75 to 90 minutes.

7. Remove from oven and allow to cool completely on a wire rack.

Serves 10

Joshna's Granola

I've made a lot of friends with this granola! It's unabashedly good for you, and totally satisfying. This is just one way to make it, so feel free to add or subtract things according to what you like and what's available to you. This recipe is a bit of an investment in high-quality ingredients, but the final product is a thing of beauty and completely worth it.

Ingredients

6 cups rolled oats

2 cups wheat germ

2 cups bran-bud cereal (like All-Bran or Grape-Nuts)

½ cup flaxseeds

¼ cup sesame seeds

2 tbsp ground cinnamon

1 large pinch salt

2 cups shredded coconut

3 cups whole almonds, or any other nut

¾ cup liquid honey

½ cup vegetable oil

½ cup maple syrup

½ cup warm water

4 cups dried fruit (a mixture of raisins, cranberries, apricots, etc.)

Method

1. Preheat oven to 375°F. In a large mixing bowl, combine oats, wheat germ, bran buds, flaxseeds, sesame seeds, cinnamon, salt, coconut and nuts. In a small saucepan, mix together honey, vegetable oil, maple syrup and water and heat until mixture is almost boiling. Add to dry ingredients and mix well. Your mixture should be sticky and crumbly.

2. Spread granola in a single layer on a parchment-lined baking sheet (use 2 sheets if necessary). Toast for about 30 minutes, stirring every few minutes so you get a nice even golden colour and your kitchen smells wonderful. You may need to cook the granola longer — keep toasting and stirring until you're happy with it.

3. Remove from oven and allow to cool completely. Crumble with your hands to create bite-size pieces. Add dried fruit to granola and toss lightly to combine.

4. Store in an airtight container for up to 2 weeks. Serve with yogurt and fresh fruit.

Makes about 12 cups

Apple Walnut Muffins

These healthy muffins include whole grains, fresh fruit and unrefined sugar. We serve them for breakfast, to rave reviews.

Ingredients

¾ cup whole wheat flour

½ cup spelt flour

1½ tsp baking powder

½ tsp baking soda

½ tsp cinnamon

½ tsp ground allspice

¼ tsp freshly grated nutmeg

¼ tsp salt

2 large eggs

1 cup packed brown sugar

½ cup plus 3 tablespoons vegetable oil

1 cup unsweetened applesauce

1 cup coarsely chopped pecans or walnuts (3½ oz/90 g)

Method

1. Place oven rack in middle position and preheat oven to 400°F. Line muffin pan with paper liners and set aside.

2. In a bowl, stir together flours, baking powder, baking soda, spices and salt. Whisk together eggs and brown sugar in a large bowl until well combined, then add oil, a little at a time, whisking until mixture is creamy. Stir in applesauce, then fold in flour mixture until flour is just moistened. Do not overmix. Stir in nuts and divide batter among muffin cups.

3. Bake until muffins are puffed and golden, about 20 minutes, and a wooden toothpick inserted in the centre of a muffin comes out clean. Cool in pan on a rack for 5 minutes, then remove muffins from pan and cool completely.

Makes 12

index

Index..

Photography credits

Laura Berman (fruit and vegetable photography)
11, 19, 50, 53, 84, 87, 123

Anna Prior (The Stop community photography)
5, 11, 12, 19, 49, 53, 87, 123

Jodi Pudge
Cover, 21, 25, 27, 33, 35, 41, 45, 47, 57, 61, 65, 67, 69, 71, 77, 79, 83, 89, 95, 97, 100, 103, 107, 117, 125, 131, 135, 139, 141, 145, 148, 151, back cover

James Tse
8, 16, 87, 120

Acknowledgments

Like anything worthwhile, this cookbook is the result of a great deal of love, hard work and devotion. Without Janet Nicol and Kirsten Hanson there would be no book. Thanks to both of them for wrapping their hearts around this project and making it possible. Thanks, too, to The Metcalf Foundation and the Wes and Mary Nicol Foundation for their generous financial support. Ruth Alves's thoughtful design, flexibility and endless patience made the book not only a collection of great recipes but also a beautiful artifact in itself. Chef Joshna Maharaj's boundless energy and creativity is infectious in person, and in print it fairly leaps off the page — we thank her for all that she has contributed to this community. We are also indebted to Sasha Chapman, a great food writer and friend, for bringing to life both The Stop's story and the journey through the seasons.

Fortunately for us, our community is home to two of the finest food photographers in Toronto: Jodi Pudge and James Tse. They embraced this project from day one and marshalled a skilled group of experts in their field to make it sing: thank you to Madeleine Johari, Lindsay Evans, Dave Picard, Angelina Dunn, Phil DeMelo and Alix Davidson. The generous team at Simon & Schuster Canada — Kevin Hanson, Felicia Quon and Alison Clarke — was also an incredible partner in this project. They believed in us, held our collective hands, opened doors and helped us create a cookbook of which we can all be very proud. Andrea Curtis, Barbara Kamienski, Sheila Scott and Lucy Waverman ensured this book holds together in grammar, measurements and prose. Finally, a sincere thanks to our community members and dedicated staff, volunteers, partner organizations and board of directors who support and safeguard our mission with diligence, wisdom and creativity.